Painting Your Home: Interiors

Julian Cassell & Peter Parham

Contents

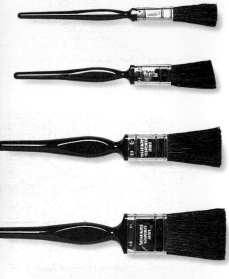

Introduction

Whether you are a complete novice or have done some decorating before, this book contains all the facts needed for painting every room of the home.

These days, there is a huge range of decorative products on the market. This can make decision-making difficult. So, to start with, 'Ideas and Choices' helps make the right choices for your particular requirements. There are suggestions and ideas for all sorts of colour schemes – from neutrals on walls to striking hues on woodwork.

It is extremely important to plan the work, and to take time to carry it out in an ordered, logical manner. 'Planning and Preparation' ensures that no part of the preparation is overlooked, as this stage is vital for achieving a good-quality finish.

The use of lining paper is often considered unnecessary by many enthusiasts. Although lining walls and/or ceilings takes extra time, it gives a flatter, more even surface that pays dividends in the end.

'Painting' aims to teach the basics to the beginner, as well as to improve the technique of the more experienced decorator. Again, ideas and alternatives are presented here to provide the widest possible range of advice on all aspects of painting.

We wish you good fortune with each process and trust that by following this book carefully, you achieve both the look you are after and the quality of finish that hard work deserves.

Ideas and Choices

The most difficult decisions when decorating are often those of choosing colours and finishes. Many people lose sleep worrying about matching the walls, ceiling and woodwork with all the furniture and the curtains. If this is your experience, try to remember that giving a room a facelift should be an enjoyable experience.

Inspiration may not come immediately, so use all available 'props' to help with decision-making. Most paint manufacturers provide tester pots and colour swatches with which you can experiment.

It may be helpful to try and find a room or style that has caught your attention in a magazine. Above all, remember that your personal taste and requirements are the most important factors.

This chapter does not attempt to push any rigid ideas, but should provide you with some options to consider on colour schemes and on the types of paint that are readily available to carry out the task.

Pale colours

Colours that are neutral and pale always give an impression of space because they reflect light more than darker colours. Rooms that do not receive much natural light can look airier when they have pale walls and ceilings, and some rooms may look less cluttered than they otherwise might.

The most common application of this principle is when ceilings are painted white to 'raise' the height of a room.

Pale colours also tend to be popular because it is easier to match furnishings with such neutral tones than with bolder, more vibrant ones.

◀ Pale pastel colours tend to be calming, and produce a relaxed, comfortable atmosphere. Shades of peach or apricot add warmth to this room. The pale slate blue provides a note of contrast, but because it is of a similar intensity to the wall colour, the overall tone is still restful.

◀ Pale hues provide perfect backdrops for favourite furnishings, ornaments or displays.

▲ Bright yellow, while not a neutral colour, adds life to what might otherwise be a dull, unwelcoming area. Other primary colours produce a similar effect in lifting the 'mood' of a room.

◀ Greens and blues are considered cool colours, providing a fresh yet soothing atmosphere. The lighter the shade, the more the walls will tend to recede, giving the impression of space.

Pictures or paintings will also stand out against a light background.

Dark colours

Dark colours are always a bold choice, but they can add considerable character to flat and lifeless surfaces and accentuate features within a room. Dark colours may create a slightly enclosed feeling, appearing to bring high ceilings down and making wall surfaces advance rather than recede. This effect can be used to create a cosy, relaxed feeling, especially in rooms used principally in the evening.

Dark colours may seem too daring for many of us. To counteract this, try using them on woodwork, so they will not be as overpowering as on a large wall surface. Furthermore, it is often wiser to use a colour one or two shades lighter than your original choice, as the colour will always seem darker once applied, especially on a large area.

▲ The deep brick red on the rear walls of the shelving complements the green perfectly, and creates a further dimension to the decoration.

◄ The dark forest green of this woodwork stands out magnificently against the pale yellow walls, emphasising the shape of the bookshelves and providing an ideal showcase for both ornaments and books.

◄ Dark blues are perceived to be cool colours which often steers people away from using them.

▼ Subtle lighting, however, may change the appearance of colours dramatically. Here, the blue on these walls displays this principle perfectly.

◄ Rich, dark red enhances the natural beauty of wood and adds a certain opulence to extravagant soft furnishings. By keeping the window bay white, the maximum amount of natural light is allowed into the room.

Paint finishes

Almost all paints suitable for the interior of houses can be divided into two broad categories: water-based and solvent-based.

Water-based paints have increased in popularity over recent years, mainly because they are easy to use and are environmentally friendly. Solvent-based paints are more traditional. They are predominantly based on white spirit and are less user friendly than their water-based counterparts.

	PRODUCT DESCRIPTION	SUITABLE SURFACES
PRIMER	Watery, dilute appearance specifically formulated to seal bare surfaces.	All bare wood, plaster or metal. Use specific primer for each surface. All-purpose primers are available.
PRIMER-UNDERCOAT	A primer and undercoat in one, providing base for top coat(s).	Bare wood.
UNDERCOAT	Dull, opaque finish providing ideal base for application of top coat(s).	Any primed surface.
MATT EMULSION	All purpose matt-finish paint. Water-based.	Plaster surfaces.
VINYL EMULSION	Available in a number of finishes from matt to silk with manufacturer's variation in texture. Water-based.	On primed or previously painted plaster surfaces, or direct to lining paper.
EGGSHELL	Mid-sheen finishing paint. Proprietary variations on this theme.	Any primed or undercoated surface.
GLOSS	Shiny 'polished' finishing paint.	Any undercoated surface, ideally wood or metal.
TEXTURED PAINT	Textured relief paint, that can be used as a finish or overpainted according to personal taste.	Plaster surfaces.
FLOOR PAINT	Finishing paint for floors.	Ideal for concrete. Can be used on brick, cement, wood and stone.
VARNISH	Translucent natural wood finish available in gloss, semi-gloss or matt, totally sealing surface.	All bare wood. May be applied over most previously stained surfaces. Water-based excellent for floors.
STAIN	Deep penetrating natural wood finish. Variety of sheens available.	All bare wood. Darker colours may be applied over previously stained surfaces.
WAX	'Natural' polished finish for wood.	All bare wood. Some proprietary waxes may require the wood to be sealed before application.
OIL	Penetrating natural wood treatment.	All bare wood, although hardwoods (eg oak, ash) produce the best finishes.

Apart from these, there are some proprietary paints that need specific handling and application techniques. Remember to pay particular attention to the manufacturer's guidelines in such cases. The table below provides all the information you may need about the majority of paint and wood finishes, both water- and solvent-based.

Always read the manufacturer's guidelines for each product as there may be small variations in the categories outlined below.

MAIN QUALITIES	LIMITATIONS	APPLICATION METHOD
Excellent sealer enabling application of further coats of paint.	Only use on bare surfaces.	Brush. May use roller or spray with water-based primers.
Easy to use, and time-saving.	Not as hard-wearing as oil-based undercoat.	Brush, roller or spray.
Hard wearing.	Application takes longer than primer-undercoat.	Brush or roller.
A thinned first coat acts as an excellent primer. Subsequent full strength coats may then be applied for finishing.	Not hardwearing.	Brush, roller or spray.
Vinyl qualities make it easy to clean.	When 'cutting in' with dark colours, framing effect is often difficult to avoid.	Brush, roller or spray.
More hardwearing than emulsions.	Slight sheen tends to accentuate imperfections on large surface areas.	Brush or roller; spray with water-based.
Very hard-wearing decorative finish. Easy to clean.	Application takes longer than most other paints, and a sound technique is required to produce the desired finish.	Brush or roller.
Adds further decorative dimension to flat walls or ceilings. Excellent for hiding rough surfaces.	Difficult to clean textured wall surfaces. Difficult to remove if redecoration required.	Roller, brush, combs/variety of finishing tools.
Hardwearing decorative finish for what would otherwise be a dull dusty surface. Easy to clean.	Colour choice often limited. Only for use on floors. New concrete may need to be left for up to 6 months before painting.	Brush or roller.
Very hard-wearing, durable and easy to clean.	Solvent-based are liable to yellow with age.	Brush, roller or spray.
Hardwearing. Enhances the grain and features of natural wood.	Difficult to strip or change colour once applied, so care is needed in initial choices.	Brush.
Accentuates natural beauty of wood; depth and quality of finish is improved over time with further applications.	Regular applications needed to maintain finish.	Brush and/or cloth. Cloth for buffing off.
Can be used mainly as a nourishing preservative or provide a polished finish.	Regular applications required. Extra care required when disposing of cloths as some oils are highly combustible.	Brush and/or cloth. Cloth for removing surplus.

Order of work

It is vital to use the correct order and system of application for whatever finish you have chosen. The illustrations below show the products required for each particular finish and the order in which they should be applied. Remember that missing out a stage will inevitably affect the quality of the finish.

WATER-BASED PAINT ON NEW PLASTER

1 Bare plaster
2 Dilute matt-emulsion primer coat
3 First coat of finishing paint
4 Top coat of finishing paint
Apply further coats if required

WATER-BASED PAINT ON LINING PAPER

1 Bare plaster
2 PVA sealer or size
3 Lining paper
4 Finishing paint: two to three coats

WATER-BASED vs SOLVENT-BASED: THE PROS AND CONS

	WATER-BASED	SOLVENT-BASED	COMMENTS
EASE OF APPLICATION	• • • • •	• • •	Water-based tend to be much easier to apply, with less 'brushing out' required.
DRYING TIME	• • • • •	•	Much quicker turn-around between coats with water-based paints.
LOW ODOUR/TAINT	• • • • •	•	White-spirit smell of solvent-based paints can be overpowering. Minimal problem with water-based.
WASHABILITY	• • •	• • • • •	Surfaces painted with solvent-based paints are easiest to clean.
DURABILITY	• • •	• • • • •	Solvent-based are more hard-wearing, although water-based are catching up with improved formulation.
BRUSHMARKS	• •	• • • •	More evident in water-based, although improving all the time.
COLOUR RETENTION	• • • •	• • •	White solvent-based (especially) tends to yellow with age.
CLEANING TOOLS	• • • • •	•	Water-based easily cleaned with water and mild detergent. Solvent-based is a lengthier process requiring white spirit.
USER-FRIENDLY	• • • •	•	All health and safety guidelines make water-based products a better option than their solvent-based counterparts.

WATER-BASED PAINT ON WOOD

1 Bare wood
2 Knotter on bare knots
3 Primer-undercoat
4 Second primer-undercoat for improved finish, or apply first coat of eggshell if top coat is going to be eggshell
5 Top coat: gloss or eggshell

OIL-BASED PAINT ON WOOD

1 Bare wood
2 Knotter on bare knots
3 Primer
4 Undercoat: apply two coats for improved finish
5 Top coat: gloss
   If using eggshell, apply two coats directly on top of primer; undercoat is not necessary

VARNISH

1 Bare wood
2 Wood dye or stain: optional, to colour wood
3 Varnish: two coats if water-based. Thinned primer coat and at least two top coats required if solvent-based

WAX

1 Bare wood
2 Wood dye: optional, to colour wood
3a Light-coloured wax: two coats for finishing, or
3b Darker wax: two coats for finishing

STAIN

1 Bare wood
2 First coat of stain: proprietary primer coat may be required
3 Second coat of stain
4 Third coat of stain, depending on shade and depth of colour required

OIL

1 Bare wood
2 First coat of oil
3 Second coat of oil: apply further coats depending on absorption of wood

Planning and Preparation

Successful decoration depends on careful planning and thorough preparation. You need to make decisions about what is required to complete the job and how to go about it. Being methodical at this early stage will save time later, as not having the right tools or running out of materials half-way through a project can be very stressful. Preparation of surfaces is vital; it is all the initial hard work, rather than the final coat of paint, that will determine the quality of the finish. Even though modern-day materials are more refined than ever before, the result will be disappointing if preparation is poor.

This chapter contains

Tools

When choosing and purchasing tools and equipment, always opt for quality rather than quantity. A few well-selected, superior items will be far more useful than buying cheap 'all-in-one' kits. These often contain many articles that you will never use.

When assembling tools, it is not necessary to purchase the complete range as listed here. Instead, buy for your specific needs and build up your equipment gradually. Also, if you have limited use for an item, especially the more expensive ones such as steam strippers, it may be more sensible to consider hiring rather than an outright purchase.

BASIC TOOLBOX FOR PREPARATION

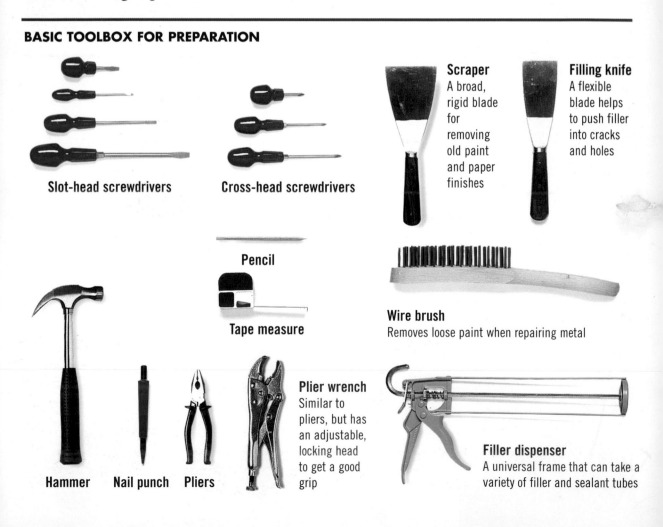

Slot-head screwdrivers

Cross-head screwdrivers

Scraper
A broad, rigid blade for removing old paint and paper finishes

Filling knife
A flexible blade helps to push filler into cracks and holes

Pencil

Tape measure

Wire brush
Removes loose paint when repairing metal

Hammer **Nail punch** **Pliers**

Plier wrench
Similar to pliers, but has an adjustable, locking head to get a good grip

Filler dispenser
A universal frame that can take a variety of filler and sealant tubes

Access and protection

Step-ladder

Dust sheet

Trestles and plank
Make a sturdy platform when working on ceilings or high walls

---

Personal protection

Protective gloves
Waterproof, to keep irritants off hands

Goggles
Keep dust, spray and chemicals out of eyes

Dust masks
(disposable)

Respirator mask
Protection against very fine dust and fumes

Stripping and sanding

Electric sander
For large areas

Electric hot-air gun
For stripping paint or varnish

Steam stripper
For fast wallpaper stripping

PAPER-HANGING TOOLS

Pasting table

Bucket

Sponge

Measuring jug

Pasting brush

Paper-hanging brush
Smooths hung paper to expel bubbles, etc

Paper-hanging scissors
Long blades help to cut straight edges

Spirit level

Steel rule

Craft knife

Craft knife with snap-off blades

Plumb line
Indicates an exact vertical

Chalk line
Marks a long, straight line where distance is too long for a steel rule

Seam roller
Presses joins flat, when hanging paper

PAINTING TOOLS
Paint preparation

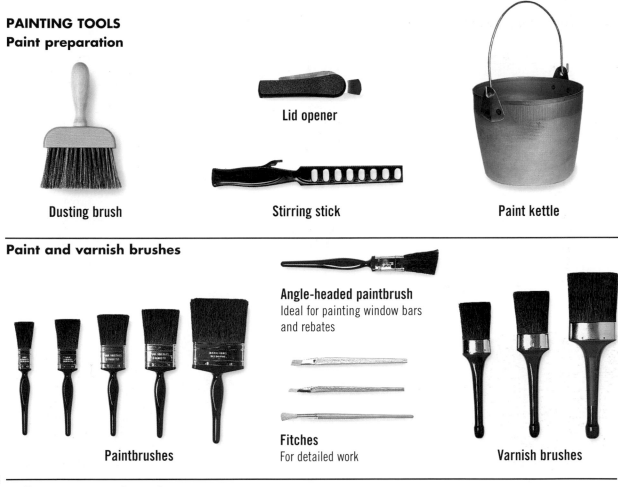

Dusting brush

Lid opener

Stirring stick

Paint kettle

Paint and varnish brushes

Angle-headed paintbrush
Ideal for painting window bars
and rebates

Fitches
For detailed work

Paintbrushes

Varnish brushes

Rollers, paint pads and sprayers

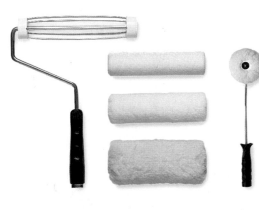

Paint pads

Roller cage and roller sleeves
Different sizes and textures of sleeve
will fit on the same roller cage

Corner roller

Roller tray

Airless spray gun

Identifying problems

Before starting any preparation, the room must first be cleared of obstacles. It is best to remove all the furniture, accessories and soft furnishings, and to take up the carpet at this stage, if it is to be replaced. If it is not possible to totally clear the room, place everything in the middle and cover with dust sheets. You are now able to get a clear view of any problem areas, decide how to treat them and to assess the extent of redecoration required. The problems outlined below are commonplace in many homes. All of them need attention before any decoration is carried out.

DAMP AND MOULD

Mould is caused by moisture build-up, usually as a result of poor ventilation. Wash it down with fungicide. Extensive mould growth should be looked at by a professional as there may be a general damp problem that needs to be solved before redecoration can take place. Old stains, caused by damp that has dried out, can be covered with proprietary sealers.

CRACKED/CHIPPED WOODWORK

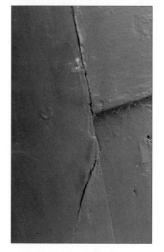

Results from general wear and tear. Depending on its extent, woodwork will need to be stripped totally or just filled and sanded before it is repainted (see pages 34–35).

WRINKLED PAPER

Commonly found in corners where the walls are not quite square and poor paper adhesion, plus slight movement in the building , has lifted and possibly torn the paper. Small areas can be cut out with a scraper, refilled and painted over.

BLEEDING KNOTS

Caused by resin weeping from a live knot, usually in relatively new timber. Strip back and seal (see pages 28–29).

POWDERY WALL SURFACES

Found in older houses that were previously painted with a type of paint called distemper, or may just be due to the breakdown of old plaster. Wash down and seal (see pages 36–37).

FLAKING TEXTURED FINISHES

Caused by water penetration (such as a burst pipe) or a poorly prepared surface. Small areas can be patched. With larger areas, the whole surface must be stripped back and the finish reapplied.

FLAKY PAINT

Caused by moisture underneath the painted surface, or where the paint has been unable to stick to a powdery or incompatible surface. (See left, and Sealing on pages 36–37.)

UNEVEN PAPERED SURFACES

Generally found in older properties. If the paper is basically sound or an overall 'rustic' finish is acceptable, do not strip as the plaster underneath may come away from the wall.

EFFLORESCENCE

Results from crystallisation of salts found in building materials. Use a scraper to remove deposits until no more appear. Repaint with water-based paint, which allows drying out to continue through the painted surface.

LIFTING WALLPAPER SEAMS

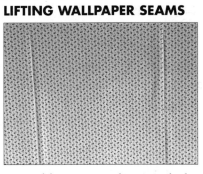

Caused by poor application, lack of paste adhesion due to damp, or simply ageing. Small areas of lining paper can be stuck back down with border adhesive. With larger areas, the whole room should be stripped and repapered.

BUBBLING PAPER

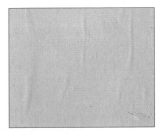

This is caused by inexpert papering or poor adhesion. The only solution is to strip and repaper the problem area (see pages 26–27).

CRACKS IN PLASTER

Caused by drying out, building settlement and general wear and tear. Fill and allow to dry out completely before painting or papering (see pages 30–31).

Paint and materials

When buying materials – and most importantly, paint – spending a little more on good-quality products will save both time and money in the long run. It is a false economy to apply four or five coats of a cheap paint when a slightly more expensive counterpart will do the job in two coats. Remember to be selective with your requirements for the particular job in hand, as many of the items on this page have only a limited shelf life.

BASIC SUPPLIES
Fillers

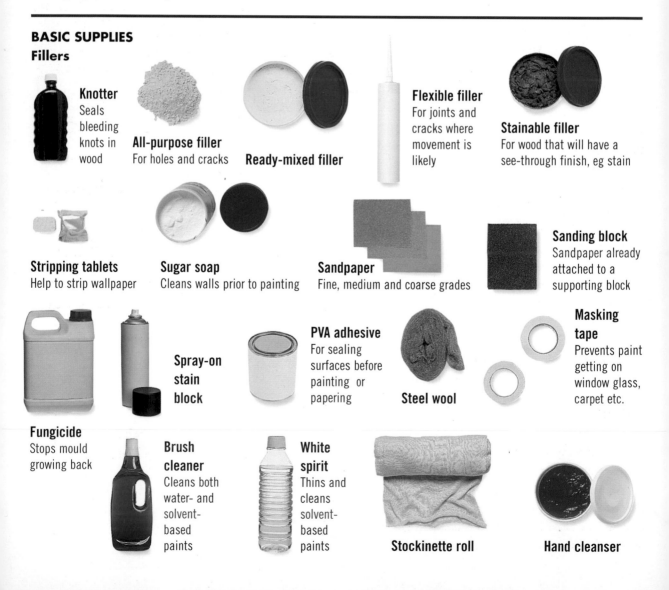

Knotter
Seals bleeding knots in wood

All-purpose filler
For holes and cracks

Ready-mixed filler

Flexible filler
For joints and cracks where movement is likely

Stainable filler
For wood that will have a see-through finish, eg stain

Stripping tablets
Help to strip wallpaper

Sugar soap
Cleans walls prior to painting

Sandpaper
Fine, medium and coarse grades

Sanding block
Sandpaper already attached to a supporting block

Fungicide
Stops mould growing back

Spray-on stain block

PVA adhesive
For sealing surfaces before painting or papering

Steel wool

Masking tape
Prevents paint getting on window glass, carpet etc.

Brush cleaner
Cleans both water- and solvent-based paints

White spirit
Thins and cleans solvent-based paints

Stockinette roll

Hand cleanser

LINING

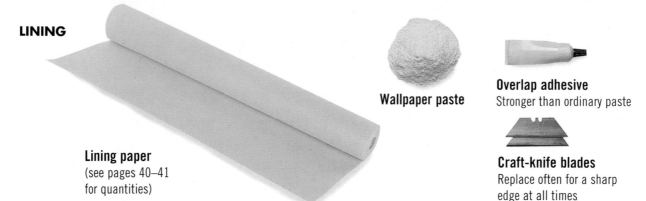

Wallpaper paste

Overlap adhesive
Stronger than ordinary paste

Lining paper
(see pages 40–41
for quantities)

Craft-knife blades
Replace often for a sharp
edge at all times

FINISHING

Primer
Undercoat
Top coat: matt,
eggshell or
gloss

Stain
Varnish
Wax
Oil
Wood dye

CAUTION
Some materials contain hazardous
chemicals. Always remember to read
the manufacturers' guidelines before
handling them.

COVERAGE

To estimate quantities, it is first necessary to measure the various surface areas. Walls and ceilings are relatively straightforward, and the same method as used for measuring up for lining paper may be used (see pages 40–41).

When calculating how much paint is needed for a window, measure it as you would a door by multiplying the height by the width. Do not deduct the glass area as this will compensate for the intricate areas of the window which make its actual surface area larger than it would appear (However, with picture windows a deduction should be made).

The table on the right can only give an approximate guide to how much paint is needed as some surfaces are more porous than others. These figures are calculated for surfaces of average porosity. Each manufacturer will produce slight variations on coverage, so it is best to take their estimates into account when buying the paint.

ACRYLIC/WATER-BASED

	sq m/litre	sq yd/gallon
Gloss	15	82
Eggshell	15	82
Emulsion	15	82
Primer/undercoat	12	65
Varnish	10	55

SOLVENT/OIL-BASED

Gloss	17	92
Eggshell	16	87
Undercoat	15	82
Primer	13	71
Varnish	15	82
Wood stain	22	120

Stripping paper

This is a time-consuming job, but with the correct methods it is reasonably straightforward. A steam stripper, which can be hired quite cheaply, speeds up the process. When using it, always wear rubber gloves and goggles as boiling water and steam can spit out from the sides of the stripping pad. If a steam stripper is not available, soak the paper with hot water or use a stripping-tablet solution instead. Gloves and goggles are still required as most stripping chemicals will irritate the skin.

TOOLS: Gloves, goggles, steam stripper, measuring jug, scraper, bucket, stirring stick, 130mm (5in) brush, wallpaper spiker or orbital scorer

MATERIALS: Stripping tablets, water

STEAM STRIPPING

1 When using a steam stripper always read the instructions. Check that the steam stripper is turned off at its power source, then pour water into its reservoir. Warm water will reduce the time needed for the stripper to boil. Then switch on the power and wait for the water to boil. Never leave a steam stripper unattended when it is switched on.

2 Put on your goggles and gloves. Place the stripper's steam pad firmly on the wallpaper you wish to strip, holding it in the same position, without moving, for about 30 seconds. Some brands of wallpaper stripper and some heavyweight papers may require a longer time for steaming.

3 Move the pad across the wall and using a scraper, strip off the loose, bubbling paper. Take care not to dig the end of the scraper into the wall, gouging holes in the plaster. You will soon build up a rhythm of stripping the paper with one hand while steaming the next piece of wall with the other.

STRIPPING WITH WATER

1 Measure hot water into a bucket and add the correct number of stripping tablets. Stir thoroughly until they are completely dissolved. Hot water alone can also be effective for soaking wallpaper.

2 Using a large brush, apply the solution to the paper, working from the top down. Do not soak more than a few square metres (yards) at a time or the paper will dry out before you have a chance to strip it off.

3 Allow the paper to soak for a few minutes, strip it away with a scraper. It is a good idea to clear up as you work, as otherwise the stripped paper will dry out on your dust sheets and become difficult to remove.

STRIPPING VINYL WALLPAPER

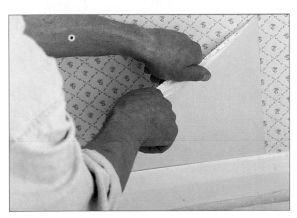

With vinyl papers, it may be possible to pull the top layer away from the backing paper, doing away with the need for a spiker/scorer. Never be tempted to leave the backing paper on the wall, however good its condition. It is rarely a sound surface on which to start decorating.

IDEAL TOOLS

Spiker

Orbital scorer

With all types of wallpaper, it is a good idea to run a wallpaper spiker or orbital scorer over the paper prior to soaking. There are several different types of spiker/scorer on the market, but all work in the same way: they aim to perforate the top layer, allowing moisture underneath the paper to aid the stripping process.

Priming and knotting

Priming is the first stage of painting a bare surface, be it wood, metal or plaster. (Plaster surfaces are covered under Sealing: see pages 36–37.) Primer provides a surface to which the following coats of paint can bond, making sure of even coverage. With wood especially, primer prevents subsequent coats of paint soaking back into the surface. Remember to choose the correct primer for each of the surfaces you are sealing.

However, before painting new or bare wood, a shellac solution, or knotter, must be painted on bare knots to seal them. This is called knotting, and prevents sap from bleeding through and discolouring later coats of paint.

TOOLS: 37mm (1½ in) paintbrush, scraper, hot-air gun, small brush for knotter

MATERIALS: Wire wool, metal primer, sandpaper, white spirit, clean cloth, knotter, wood primer

PRIMING METAL

1 Lightly rub down copper pipes with a pad of fine wire wool. This cleans off any grime and provides a key for the paint. This method can also be used if the pipes are to remain unpainted for an attractive polished finish.

2 Although it is not essential to prime copper piping, a coat of metal primer on pipes that become heated, such as central-heating radiator feeds, will help to prevent the top coat of paint from discolouring.

3 The most common ferrous-metal object in the home is a central-heating radiator. As it is a surface that gets hot, it must be painted when cold and primed with an oil-based metal primer. First, sand the corroded areas back to shiny metal. Wipe off any dust with a clean cloth and prime immediately before any oxidisation can occur.

KNOTTING AND PRIMING PREVIOUSLY PAINTED WOOD

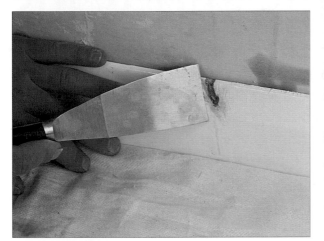

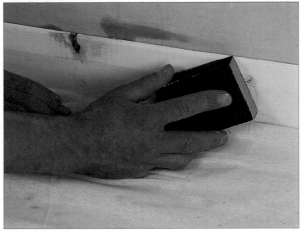

1 When treating an old bleeding knot which has discoloured the paintwork, remove the excess resin with a scraper. If the knot appears to be still active, carefully heat it with a hot-air gun, letting all the resin bubble out. Continue to scrape the area clean until no more bleeding occurs. When using a hot-air gun, follow all the precautions laid out on pages 32–33.

2 Once the knot is completely free of resin, smooth the area of wood around it with sandpaper wrapped round a sanding block. When the wood is quite smooth, take a clean cloth, moisten it with white spirit and wipe down the wood. This helps to pick up any remaining particles of wood dust or dirt, and cleans the prepared surface so that it is ready for painting.

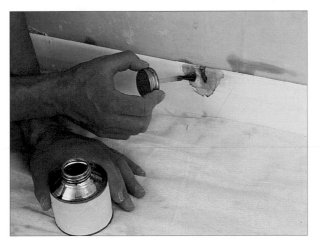

PRIMING BARE WOOD

3 Apply the knotting solution sparingly, slightly overlapping it on to the surrounding wood. Two coats are normally required for a good seal. Always allow the first to dry thoroughly before adding the second. Then patch-prime the knot area.

Work the primer along and into the grain of the wood. As primer is quite thin, apply it sparingly, otherwise runs may occur. On bare wood, make sure every area is covered, but on previously painted wood, only the bare patches need priming.

Filling ceilings and walls

Cracks and holes in plasterwork are extremely common. They are caused either by slight movement in the building structure or just everyday wear and tear. To repair these defects, there are a number of different fillers available. Flexible fillers are best used in areas of potentially high movement, such as in cracks around door architraves. Pre-mixed and fine surface fillers come ready to use in a tub. However, powder filler is by far the most common type used. It is mixed with water, as and when it is needed.

TOOLS: Dusting brush, filling knife, 25mm (1in) paintbrush, caulking blade, sanding block, hammer

MATERIALS: Powder filler, water, fine-grade sandpaper, newspaper, batten, nails

1 Use the edge of a clean filling knife or scraper to rake out and clean up the damaged area. Brush out any loose debris with a dusting brush.

2 Pour the amount of powder filler required on to a clean board. An old paint tub lid is ideal for this purpose. When estimating how much you should mix up at a time, bear in mind that the filler will remain workable for approximately one hour. Gradually add water, mixing the filler into a creamy yet firm consistency.

3 Dampen the hole and the area around it with water. This lengthens the drying time so the filler is less likely to shrink. It also helps the filler and the plaster to bond.

IDEAL TOOL

When faced with an old wall that has many small cracks, a caulking blade helps to cover a large surface area very quickly. Use it in the same manner as a filling knife. It is also excellent for wide holes as its large blade can rest on the edges of the hole, keeping the filler level.

4 Load some filler on to the filling knife and draw it across the hole, using the flexibility of the knife to firmly press the filler into the hole. You may need to draw the filling knife across the hole two or three times to ensure that the area has been covered completely and that the filler is firmly in place. Always try to fill the hole slightly 'proud' of the surrounding area, to allow for a small amounts of shrinkage. When the hole is filled, use the filling knife to clean off any excess filler from the wall around the hole to avoid any extra sanding when the filler has dried.

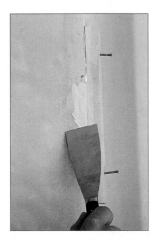

5 Sand the area when dry with a fine grade of sandpaper. Then run your fingers over the hole to check that it feels smooth and flush with the rest of the wall. If it is not, dust it off, wet as before and use a thin skim of filler to make good any indentations. With particularly deep holes, trying to fill them with just one load of filler can be difficult. Bulging will occur where the filler is unable to bond with the surrounding area. In this case, it may be necessary to use several thin coats to gradually build up the filler until it is level with the surrounding wall.

FILLING DEEP CRACKS

Sometimes it is necessary to fill a large, deep crack, perhaps in the corner of a room. Prior to filling, screw up a length of newspaper and, using a filling knife, press it very firmly into the crack. This will give the filler a base to sit on while it dries.

FILLING A CORNER

To repair an external corner, fix a length of wooden batten flush to one edge of the corner securing it in place with two nails. Fill the hole using a filling knife or caulking blade. When the filler has dried, sand the area, remove the batten and repeat the process on the adjacent corner edge. Finally, fill the four nail holes made by tacking on the batten. This technique will reproduce the original square corner edge.

Stripping wood

When wood is to be repainted it is sometimes necessary to strip off all previous coats because the paint build-up can make doors and windows stick, or simply because fine details have become obscured under several coats of paint. Before applying any natural wood finish, all traces of previous paint or varnish must be completely removed.

There are two methods of stripping woodwork: by applying chemicals or using a hot-air gun.

Ideally, doors should be taken off their hinges and laid flat on a work bench or trestles. Protective gloves and goggles are a sensible precaution, and make sure that the surrounding area is covered with dust sheets as stripping is often a very messy process.

TOOLS: Gloves, goggles, old paintbrush, scraper, shavehook, hot-air gun, filling knife, sanding block, electric sander, stiff brush

MATERIALS: Chemical stripper, white vinegar, clean cloth, stainable filler, sandpaper, white spirit, wire wool

CHEMICAL STRIPPING

1 Although some chemical strippers are mixed into a paste and applied with a scraper or spatula, the most common are painted on. Use an old paintbrush to dab the stripper lightly on the painted surface, working in areas of approximately 0.5sq m (½sq yd). Allow the stripper to react with the paint for 5 to 20 minutes, depending on the manufacturer's guidelines and the number of coats of paint to be removed.

2 Using a scraper or the flat edge of a shavehook, begin to remove the softened layers of paint. If not all the paint comes away you may need to let the chemicals react for longer before trying to strip, or further coats of stripper may be needed to remove thick layers of paint. Dispose of the stripper/paint scrapings in a sealed container so that they do not cause contamination when thrown away.

PREPARING FOR A NATURAL WOOD FINISH

3 Dust off the sanded area using a brush or a clean cloth. When it is as dust free as possible, wipe the entire surface down using a clean cloth dampened with a little white spirit. Allow to dry.

1 Cracks or defects on the stripped surface can be filled (see pages 34–35). For wood that will be finished with a natural wood treatment such as stain or varnish, it is essential to use stainable filler.

2 As always, thorough sanding is required to obtain a smooth finish. For large surface areas an electric sander saves both time and energy. Always work along the direction of the wood grain.

IDEAL TOOL

A shavehook is an ideal stripping tool as its pointed corners can be used to remove paint from the most intricate areas, such as the corners of door panels.

CLEANING DOWN

Once all the paint (or varnish) has been completely removed using chemical stripper, the wood must be cleaned down and the stripper chemicals neutralised so that they do not continue to attack the wood, or the finish that you are going to apply once the wood is back to its bare surface.

The solutions used for cleaning down depend on the solvent base of the stripper itself; so always read the manufacturer's instructions to see which treatment is specified. One method involves using ordinary white vinegar, followed by scrubbing with a stiff brush and a generous amount of clean water.

If any traces of paint remain stuck in the grain of the wood, dab a small amount of stripper on the area and rub gently with some wire wool. Once the ingrained material has been removed clean down as before.

USING A HOT-AIR GUN

When using a hot-air gun, take care not to point it at one area for too long as the heat will scorch the wood. Keep the gun moving slowly, only dwelling in one place long enough for the paint to begin bubbling. It is then ready to be scraped off.

Filling wood

When preparing wood that is to be painted over, the types of filler used for walls and ceilings are also suitable to fill cracks or holes in wood. However, if the wood is to be stained or varnished, a stainable filler must be used so that it can be coloured to match and blend in with the surrounding wood.

Powder and ready-mixed fillers are ideal for dealing with chips in paintwork or nail holes. However, for areas that might experience some slight movement, such as cracked door panels and architraves, flexible fillers are more suitable as they will tolerate slight movement.

TOOLS: Hammer, nail punch, filling knife, filler board, scraper, skeleton gun/filler dispenser

MATERIALS: Sandpaper, powder filler, flexible filler

POWDER FILLER

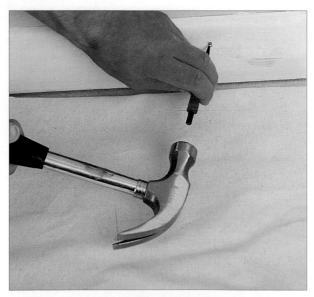

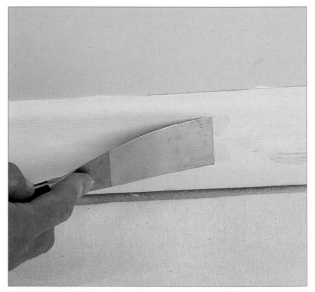

1 Before starting to fill wood areas, such as a skirting board, always check for any protruding nails. They will spoil the overall finish and may cause an injury when the wood is sanded. Use a nail punch and hammer to drive nails into and just below the surface of the wood.

2 Fill the hole slightly proud using a filling knife. Then wet the blade of the knife and draw it across the filled area, smoothing the filler to help reduce the amount of sanding needed. When the filler has dried, sand the wood back to a smooth finish.

FLEXIBLE FILLER

  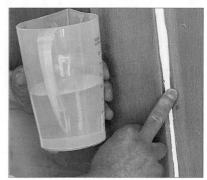

1 When filling a cracked joint, rake out any loose paint or dust using the sharp edge of a scraper. Sand the area smooth and use a dusting brush to clear away the debris.

2 Cut the nozzle of the filler tube to the size required. Gently pull the dispenser trigger while drawing the end of the nozzle down the crack, squeezing the filler into the gap.

3 Run a wetted finger over the filler, pushing it into the recess and creating a smooth finish. It is important to smooth the filler soon after it is applied as it dries out very quickly.

3 If bubbles and flaking on an old painted surface are extensive, you may need to strip off all the paint back to the bare wood (see pages 32–33). However, in a small area, simply shave off all the loose material using a scraper, taking care not to dig into the wood itself.

4 Sand down the area with a medium-grade sandpaper or block. Then use a fine-grade paper to feather the edges of the bare wood with the surrounding painted area. If the indentation is still noticeable, skim with a thin layer of filler and sand to a smooth finish when dry.

Cleaning down and sealing

Both these processes are vital in order to stabilise wall surfaces before any sort of decoration takes place. Either painting or papering over unstable or dirty areas may look acceptable at first, but the finish will inevitably deteriorate before long.

Although these all-important initial steps cannot be seen when the decorating is completed, they are absolutely essential for a good-quality and long-lasting finish.

TOOLS: Bucket, stirring stick, gloves, sponge, 37, 100 and 125mm (1½, 4 and 5in) paintbrushes

MATERIALS: PVA adhesive, emulsion paint, damp sealant or oil-based undercoat, aerosol stain block, sugar soap, water

CLEANING DOWN

1 Ceilings, walls and woodwork should be cleaned down using a solution of sugar soap or mild detergent. Mix with warm water as per the manufacturer's instructions.

2 Wear protective gloves when using sugar soap as it irritates the skin. Make sure you clean all surfaces thoroughly, removing any dust and impurities.

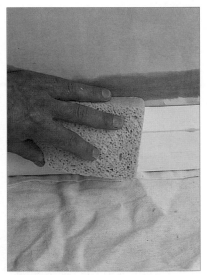

3 The sugar soap solution must be rinsed off every surface, using plenty of clear water and a sponge. Once it is quite clean, allow the surface to dry completely before continuing to decorate.

SEALING

1 Once all surfaces have been prepared and cleaned down, PVA adhesive is ideal for sealing all porous or dusty surfaces. Primers can also be used, but on large areas they will take longer to apply and tend to be less economic. A coat of PVA solution provides both a sound surface for painting or acts as a 'size' if you are going to use lining paper. Read the manufacturer's guidelines for mixing, but as a rule 1 part PVA to 5 parts water is the standard dilution required.

2 Apply the PVA solution liberally, making sure of good coverage. 'Pick up' and brush in any drips or runs that may occur. When dry, run your hand over the surface to check whether it is still dusty or powdery. If so, add a second coat.

3 New plaster surfaces can also be primed or sealed in a number of ways. Water-based products are the easiest option. If you are going to paint directly on top of the plaster, diluted white emulsion is ideal for two reasons. First, because emulsion is permeable, any remaining moisture in the plaster can dry through the emulsion. Second, this will give a more uniform wall colour and will save having to apply more coats of paint than is absolutely necessary. Again, ensure good coverage when applying. (See Using a Brush, pages 70–71, if you have any problems.)

COVERING DAMP STAINS

Damp stains are common, but can be cured with the correct treatment. Consult a professional if a damp patch is clearly active as you may have an exterior problem that needs attention. If the stain is old and dry, or the problem has been cured, apply a proprietary damp sealant or an oil-based undercoat over the area.

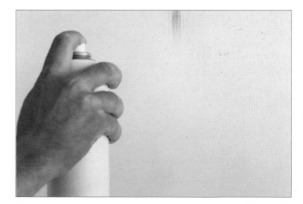

Some nondescript stains keep persisting through paintwork. Proprietary aerosol stain blocks will generally take care of marks that are the most difficult to cover.

Lining

Whether you are eventually going to paint or wallpaper a room, using lining paper on walls and ceilings makes all the difference for a professional rather than an amateur finish. Lining paper smooths out imperfections and gives an ideal surface on which to decorate.

There is a commonly held belief that you must line horizontally before wallpapering, and vertically for painting purposes. The choice is a purely practical one, however: the aim is to cover the ceiling and/or walls with the fewest number of lengths, to make best use of time and effort.

This chapter will show you how to approach lining a room using the correct techniques, and how to overcome any problems that you may encounter.

Preparation

Before starting to hang any lining paper, decide how many rolls are needed to complete the job. Using a tape measure and the table on the right, you can be surprisingly accurate.

The diagram to the right illustrates the best way to calculate surface areas. There is no right or wrong place to start, as each surface should be treated as separate to the next. Mentally divide your room into different areas (see below right) and decide on the most practical direction to line; this will help you decide your order of work. Begin with the ceiling as it is, in fact, easier than most walls because there are fewer obstacles to work around.

When lining a wall horizontally, start at the top and work down, as working from the bottom up may cause problems when joining the paper at higher levels, especially after papering around an obstacle such as a doorway, window or fireplace.

TOOLS: Tape measure, pocket calculator, bucket, measuring jug, stirring stick

MATERIALS: Lining paper, packet of wallpaper paste, water

1 When setting out equipment it is important to be well organised. Place the buckets of paste and clean water under the table to save space and to avoid accidents. Always keep your table clean and clear of obstacles. Try to keep everything to hand to save time and energy.

2 When mixing up paste ensure all the equipment is clean. Always read the manufacturer's instructions as they can vary between different brands of paste. Measure out the correct quantity of cold water using a measuring jug.

3 Start to stir the water, then sprinkle the powder slowly into the bucket. Continue to stir for 2 minutes after adding all the paste. Leave it to stand for another 3 minutes, then stir again to ensure there are no lumps. It is now ready to use.

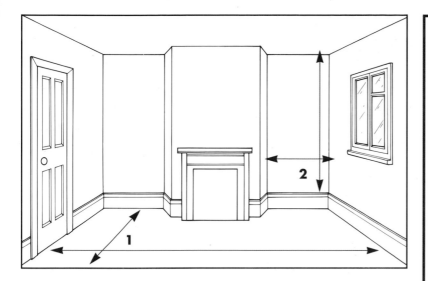

ROLLS OF LINING PAPER NEEDED

Total Surface Area to Line		No of rolls
sq m	sq yd	
5	6	1
10	12	2
15	18	3

For every additional 5sq m (6sq yd), add one roll of lining paper.

Standard roll of lining paper is 56cm x 10.05m = 5.628sq m (22in x 11yd = 6¾sq yd). The excess of 0.628sq m (¾sq yd) per roll allows for both trimming and wastage.

If you are not using standard rolls, simply work out the surface area of the rolls you are using and create your own table by the same method as above.

MEASURING UP

1 Measure these two lengths and multiply together to calculate the area of the ceiling.

2 Measure these two lengths and multiply together to calculate the area of the wall to the right of the chimney breast. Use the same technique to work out the area of all other walls.

Do not deduct anything for obstacles such as doors and windows, as you will need to compensate for wastage when trimming during application of the paper.

ORDER OF WORK

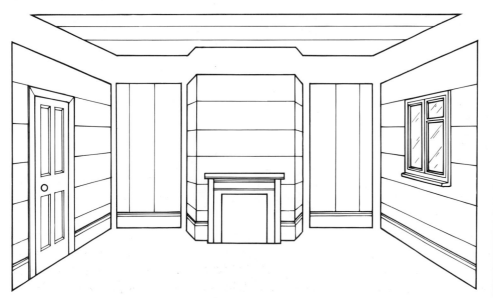

DOUBLE LINING

On particularly uneven wall surfaces, the final finish may look better if you apply two layers of lining paper before painting. Ensure that the joins on the second layer do not coincide with seams on the first.

Cutting and pasting

When cutting lengths of lining paper always add 10cm (4in) to your basic measurement to allow a 5cm (2in) overlap at each end for final trimming.

    After pasting, leave the paper for about 5 minutes for the paste to soak into the paper. This makes it less likely to bubble, more pliable and easier to work with. Once you start work it is advisable to write a number on each length: you may have up to three or four lengths soaking at any one time, and this will keep them in the correct order.

TOOLS: Pasting table, tape measure, pencil, steel rule, scissors, pasting brush, paper-hanging brush, sponge

MATERIALS: Lining paper, bucket of wallpaper paste, water

1 Carefully unroll the lining paper along the length of the pasting table. If long pieces of paper are going to be needed, gently fold the paper back on itself along the table. Use a tape measure to work out the length of paper required. Make a pencil mark in the centre of the paper where the first piece is to be cut.

2 Keep the edges of the length of paper flush with the edges of the table. This will help to ensure a square cut. Place a straight edge at the pencil mark, check it is square and draw a line along its length.

3 Cut a neat, straight line along the pencil line. Then lie the paper flat along the table with the excess paper falling over one end. Use the paper-hanging brush to hold the other end of the paper still.

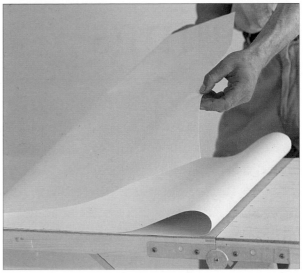

4 Line up the paper flush with the edges of the table, to avoid getting paste on the face of the paper. Apply the paste evenly, working from the centre outwards, ensuring the whole area is covered.

5 Once the paper on the table is pasted, gently fold the pasted end over, starting a concertina. Pull this along to one end of the table, again with the paper-hanging brush anchoring the other end.

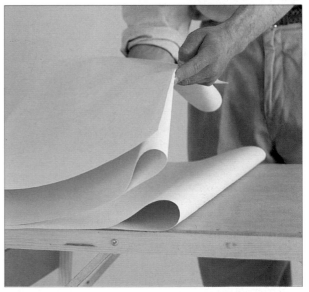

6 Continue to paste the remaining paper, working up to the end of the table. Always make sure that the paste is applied evenly, and that all areas of the paper are covered with paste. Try to avoid getting any paste on the other (unpasted) side of the paper.

7 Keep folding the paper back on itself to make up a finished concertina. When all the paper has been pasted, remove it from the table and leave it to soak for the required time. Wipe the table down with a slightly damp sponge to clean up any excess paste.

Ceilings

Always try to line across the longest dimension of the room as fewer lengths will be required, and this will save time.

Make sure that you have a solid platform from which to work. Trestles and planks are ideal as they enable you to get close to the wall–ceiling junction at both ends of the platform. Adjust its height so that the top of your head is 25–30cm (9–12in) from the ceiling.

Lining the ceiling is not as difficult as it may appear. Once the first length is hung and a straight edge established, subsequent lengths become easier and less time consuming.

TOOLS: Trestles and plank, paper-hanging brush, pencil, scissors, small brush for pasting edges, sponge

MATERIALS: Lining paper, bucket of wallpaper paste, water

1 Arrange the trestles and plank under the area where you wish to start. Carefully lay out the concertina along the plank. Pick up one end of the paper.

2 Start papering at the edge of the ceiling. Take care to keep the paper edge parallel with the length of the adjacent wall. Using the paper-hanging brush push the paper into the junction, allowing for 5cm (2in) overlap.

3 When the paper is held securely at one end, move slowly along the plank, brushing the paper from the centre out in a herringbone fashion. Keep the edge of the paper tight to the wall using it as a guide. Brush the length into position and repeat step 2 at the opposite end.

4 When the length is hung, run a pencil along where the wall and ceiling meet to make a straight line. Alternatively, run a pair of scissors along to make a crease.

EASIER CEILINGS

Papering a ceiling is easier and less tiring with two people. One can hold the paper while the other manoeuvres it into place.

5 Carefully peel back the paper. Using the paper-hanging scissors, cut a neat, straight edge along the pencil guideline or scissor crease.

6 Push the paper back into position. Work along the length, checking for bubbles or lifting at the edge. Apply extra paste to edges where needed.

7 After each length is hung, immediately wipe off any surplus paste from all the surfaces, or it will stain them.

Hang the next length in the same way as the first but place the edge of the new length adjacent to that of the first. Slide the paper into position making a neat butt join.

Walk down the plank brushing out the paper, making sure you keep the two edges of the join completely flush. Trim off at each end as before.

DEALING WITH GAPS

If the wall is not square, you will find that a gap appears along the wall–ceiling junction as you work along the length of the ceiling. A small gap of 5mm or less can be filled (see page 51), but if a larger gap appears, simply move the paper closer to the wall, allowing an overlap on to the wall. This overlap can be trimmed using the technique shown in steps 4–6 above.

Ceiling roses

Most ceilings have at least one light fitting and by far the most common is the ceiling rose. Two methods can be used to paper around them. The first, shown in steps 1–5, is to pull the pendant through a cut in the paper. The second and more reliable method, shown in the box on page 47, is to measure the distance between the starting wall and the ceiling rose to ensure that a seam between lengths will coincide with the pendant.

TOOLS: Trestles and plank, paper-hanging brush, scissors, craft knife, small brush for pasting edges, sponge, screwdriver

MATERIALS: Lining paper, bucket of wallpaper paste, water, clean cloth

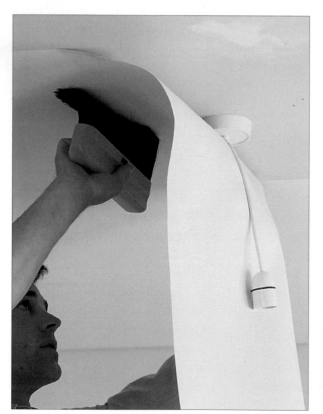

ELECTRICAL SAFETY
Always remember to turn off the power supply before undertaking any work around electrical fittings.

1 When you reach the ceiling rose with a length of pasted paper, gently brush the paper over the pendant, so that you can see where the rose is located in relation to the paper.

2 Support the unfixed side of the paper with one hand. Using scissors, carefully mark the location of the centre of the rose on the underside of the paper. Make a small cut.

3 Gently pull the pendant through the cut, taking care not to tear the paper. Then brush the remaining length of paper away, continuing on to the wall on the other side of the room.

4 Using the scissors, make a series of small cuts out to the edge of the rose. Work right round the rose, but do not cut any further than the edge of the plastic circle itself.

5 Crease around the edge of the rose and trim with a craft knife. Brush out any remaining bubbles from the entire length, and wipe off any excess paste from the pendant with a dry cloth.

METHOD 2: SEAM JOIN

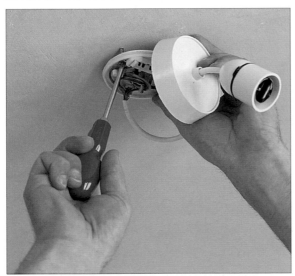

1 Turn off the power supply. Unscrew the rose's casing by hand and loosen off the retaining screws. Then allow the entire pendant to drop approximately 5cm (2in).

2 Using the paper-hanging brush, tuck in the paper edges underneath the rose. Tighten the screws and screw the ceiling rose casing back into position.

Walls

Lining paper on walls can be hung either horizontally or vertically. The choice is purely a practical one. Vertical lining is ideal for small alcoves as fewer lengths are required, whereas a long wall can be quickly covered with horizontal lengths. Vertical lining uses a vertical corner of the wall as a straight edge, whereas horizontal lining takes its guide from where the wall and the ceiling meet.

As horizontal lengths are normally longer than vertical lengths, a much larger concertina is required. To overcome this problem, make the folds smaller so that the concertina is more compact and easier to manage with one hand.

TOOLS: Trestles and plank, paper-hanging brush, pencil, scissors, craft knife, small brush for pasting edges, sponge

MATERIALS: Lining paper, bucket of wallpaper paste, water

HORIZONTAL LINING

1 Start papering at the top of the wall leaving a 5cm (2in) overlap around the corner onto the next area of wall. Line up the top edge of the paper with the wall and ceiling junction. If the wall–ceiling junction is not square, move the paper to overlap onto the ceiling and trim as usual when the remainder of the length is hung.

2 Slowly release the folds of the concertina, smoothing the paper along the wall using a paper-hanging brush. Brushing from the centre of the paper outwards, continue along to the other corner, keeping the top edge of the paper flush with the wall–ceiling junction.

3 Mark a line at the corner with a pencil, or crease the corner with scissors, then gently pull the paper away from the wall. Trim with the scissors or a craft knife.

4 Push the paper back into the corner with the brush. Extra paste may be needed if the edge of the paper has dried out during trimming. Repeat steps 3 and 4 at the other end of the length.

CROOKED ROOMS

If the wall or ceiling is very crooked (and it has been necessary to overlap paper on to the ceiling) you will be unable to use the wall–ceiling junction as a guideline to hang the entire length. So that you do not find yourself papering this first length at a sharp angle, it is wise to hold a spirit level at the bottom edge to ensure that the first length is hung straight. When lining vertically, a spirit level can also be used as a guideline when unsquare walls are causing problems.

VERTICAL LINING

1 Vertical lining is an excellent way to deal with problem areas such as pipes. Start the first length flush with the pipes and push the paper behind them so the join will be hidden.

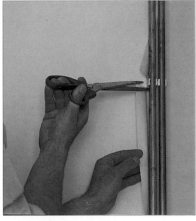

2 Mark the location of the pipe clips with a pencil and make two small cuts to the edge of the clips. Push the paper around the clips and trim off the excess paper.

3 Cut another length and butt-join it to the previously hung paper. Smooth and trim as before. Wipe any excess paste off the pipes as it will otherwise react with paint, if used.

Corners

When lining, the only corners you need to paper around are external (that is, those that stick out). At internal corners it is better to begin or end paper, because trying to bend it around the corner usually causes bubbles and problems with adhesion. Using filler on internal corners, as shown here, is a far wiser and ultimately neater option. If you have difficulty with an external corner that is uneven or not square, a manufactured butt join is the ideal solution.

TOOLS: Trestles and plank, paper-hanging brush, scissors, steel rule, craft knife, sponge

MATERIALS: Lining paper, bucket of wallpaper paste, water, flexible filler, powder filler, sandpaper, cloth

EXTERNAL CORNERS

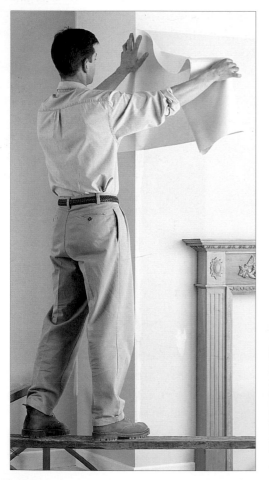

1 Approach the external corner holding the horizontal concertina in one hand. Use the other hand to push the paper up to the corner edge, keeping the horizontal edge of the length of paper flush with the edge of the ceiling or the paper above, forming a neat butt join.

2 Fold the paper around the corner using the paper-hanging brush to expel any bubbles. Make sure that the top edge of the paper is not overlapping the paper already hung above it.

3 Run your fingers gently down the corner to check for any wrinkles or creases. Smooth them out, if necessary. Once the corner is neat and problem-free, proceed along the wall with the rest of the length.

UNEVEN EXTERNAL CORNERS

 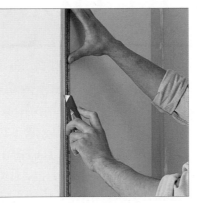 

1 For an uneven corner, bend the horizontal length around the corner and trim off all except a 5cm (2in) overlap. Do this with each (horizontal) length on the corner. Hang the next length (on the next section of wall) vertically, on top of the overlaps.

2 On the wall with the vertical length, place a straight edge 3cm (1¼in) from the corner. Using a craft knife, cut a straight line down the straight edge. Then move the straight edge and repeat the process, so continuing the cut from ceiling to skirting.

3 Pull back the paper and gently remove the excess (overlapping) strips of paper. Push the paper back into position using the paper-hanging brush. Finally, wipe the area with a damp sponge to remove any excess paste.

INTERNAL CORNERS

1 Because we recommend trimming all lengths at an internal corner, for a perfect finish, run a bead of flexible filler along all internal corners, and along the skirting board top.

2 Smooth along the filler with a wetted finger. This will neaten the finish, and prevent the edges of the paper from lifting later. Wipe off any excess filler with a clean, damp cloth.

FILLING GAPS

Small gaps between lengths are sometimes unavoidable. These can be overcome using a fine surface filler, and then sanded smooth.

Doors and obstacles

Some room features – such as door surrounds, flush windows and fireplaces – protrude out from the wall, and lining paper must be cut to fit around them. No matter what the obstacle, the technique used is much the same. A neat and exact finish is produced by precisely trimming into angles and along edges. The examples shown here include a fireplace that needs complex trimming, and a door because, quite simply, every room has one.

TOOLS: Trestles and plank, paper-hanging brush, pencil, scissors, craft knife, small brush for pasting edges, sponge

MATERIALS: Lining paper, bucket of wallpaper paste, water

FIREPLACES

1 When the paper reaches the fireplace, allow it to flap over the top corner of the mantlepiece. Make a cut diagonally towards the upper part of the corner, taking care that the paper below the cut does not tear under its own weight.

2 Having made this initial cut, ignore the paper fold on top of the fireplace for the time being. With the aid of the paper-hanging brush and scissors, push the paper gently into the angles of the mantlepiece making small right-angled cuts to allow it to lie flat on the wall.

3 Trim the small flaps with a craft knife, taking care to get as close as possible to the moulding, and without leaving any gaps. Continue to paper along the top of the mantlepiece and repeat steps 1–3 at the other corner. Then trim the fold on top of the mantlepiece.

4 It is vital to clean the excess paste off ornate obstacles immediately in order to prevent later staining or discolouration. Use a clean dampened sponge, and pay particular attention to paste that may have found its way into intricate details.

DOORS

2 Both hands now freed, feel for the corner of the architrave. Cut diagonally towards this point with scissors. Carefully draw back the excess paper hanging over the door. Using the paper-hanging brush, firmly push the paper covering the wall above the door into the edge of the architrave. Do the same with the other corner of the architrave.

1 Allow the length of paper to fall over the corner of the door architrave. Continue to hang the length along the rest of the wall, loosely attaching it to the wall surface.

3 Using a craft knife, trim away the excess paper, working carefully around the side and top edges of the door architrave.

Recessed windows

The technique for lining around a recessed window combines a number of steps already covered in this chapter. However, the order in which you hang the various lengths of paper is vital to produce the best possible finish. The particular method shown here will also come in useful when tackling similar types of shapes and obstacles, such as recessed doors or alcoves.

TOOLS: Trestles and plank, paper-hanging brush, scissors, craft knife, small brush for pasting edges, steel rule, sponge

MATERIALS: Lining paper, wallpaper paste, water

1 Hang the first length of paper horizontally, as usual, allowing the paper to span right across the recess. When you have made sure the paper is correctly butt-joined to the previous length, return to the window and make two vertical cuts approximately 1.5cm (⅝in) in from the corners of the recess. Carefully continue these cuts right up to the top edge of the window recess.

2 Starting in the middle, use the paper-hanging brush to push the flap of paper you have made back into the recess, expelling any air bubbles as you do so. Move the brush along the edge continuing the process until the paper is properly in place on the ceiling of the recess.

3 Make sure the paper has been firmly positioned in the junction between the window frame and the upper part of the recess, before trimming as usual.

4 Fold the 1.5cm (⅝in) flap around the corner of the vertical recess using your brush and fingers to expel any air bubbles if necessary. Add extra paste to the edge of the paper if it has dried out too quickly. Hang the next length, again allowing a flap of paper approximately 1.5cm (⅝in) wide to fold around into the recess. Repeat this process at the opposite side of the window recess.

5 Depending on the height of the window recess, you may need to hang further lengths of paper before finally reaching the window sill. At the sill, carefully trim the paper using a series of right-angled cuts, moulding the paper around the corner of the sill and underneath it. Once you have successfully dealt with one side, repeat this process when the paper reaches the opposite corner of the sill.

6 Measure and cut a panel of paper to finish off each vertical return of the recess. Line up the straight edge of the paper with the vertical corner, covering the trimmed overlaps of the previous lengths.

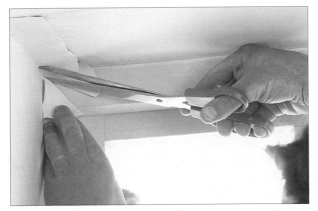

7 Make diagonal cuts into the top corner of the recess. Repeat this at the bottom corner, to assist final trimming. Any small gaps can be filled using the methods shown on page 51.

REFINING YOUR TECHNIQUE

You may find that this technique of overlapping different pieces of lining paper does not produce a completely flat surface, as the small cuts around the vertical, external corners of the recess may form an impression in the paper pasted over the top. Faced with this problem, there are two points to consider. First, it is likely that curtains will eventually cover these imperfections. Second, as you become more skilled, you may prefer to try the manufactured butt-join technique shown in Uneven External Corners (see page 51).

Electrical wall fittings

It goes without saying that light switches and electrical sockets are very common features on walls. It often appears to be difficult to paper around them neatly but if care is taken, they need not present a problem. It is important to make a neat job of light switches as every time you enter or leave a room, your eyes are naturally drawn towards them. Whatever their size or shape, the technique for coping with them remains the same.

Always remember to turn off the electricity at the mains or consumer unit before working near any electrical fitting.

TOOLS: Trestles and plank, paper-hanging brush, pencil, scissors, screwdriver, craft knife, small brush for pasting edges, sponge

MATERIALS: Lining paper, bucket of wallpaper paste, water, dry cloth

1 Turn off the electricity at the mains. Paper directly over the top of the power point or switch, butt-joining the paper, as usual.

2 Brush gently over the fixture, allowing it to form an impression in the paper. Take care not to tear the paper when carrying out this step.

3 Holding the paper firmly over the switch or power point, make a small diagonal pencil mark, 5mm (¼in) in from each of its corners.

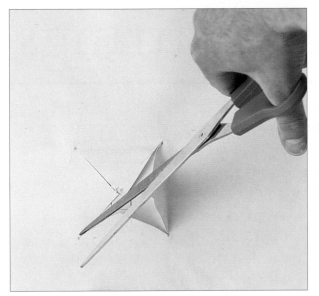

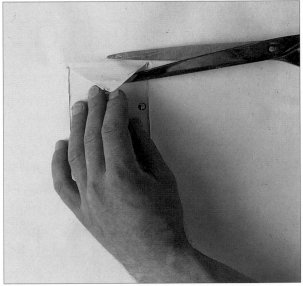

4 Using scissors, carefully make four diagonal cuts from the centre of the switch out to the pencil marks.

5 Trim off each of the four flaps, just inside the outer edge of the switch, so that a small amount of overlap remains over the switch plate.

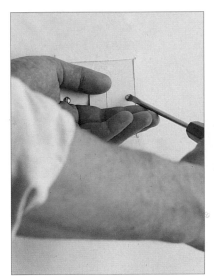

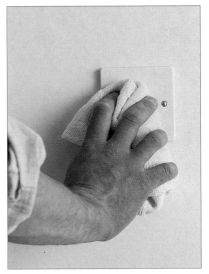

6 Unscrew the two retaining screws that hold the face plate on to the switch itself. It is not necessary to unscrew them completely, but just far enough to move the face plate a little way out from the wall.

7 Ease the face plate out from the wall, rotating it slightly from side to side. Be careful when pushing the face plate through the paper as erratic movements will tear it. Use the brush to push the paper behind the plate.

8 Wipe off any excess paste with a dry cloth. Put the face plate back and tighten up the screws, making sure the small paper flaps are firmly tucked behind the face plate. Take care not to over-tighten the screws.

Wall-mounted fittings

It is difficult to paper around wall-mounted fittings such as lights and central-heating radiators, and it is usually best to remove them. However, removing a radiator may be problematic due to old pipework and connections that have seized up. Wall lights should be easy to take down, but if they prove difficult to move, be careful to keep paste off brass and other fittings as it will quickly tarnish them. Obviously, papering around electrical fittings is best done during daylight hours when it is easy to see with the power turned off.

TOOLS: Screwdriver, scissors, pencil, paper-hanging brush, radiator roller, small brush for pasting edges, sponge

MATERIALS: Insulating tape, lining paper, bucket of wallpaper paste, water

LIGHT FITTINGS

1 Remember to turn off the electricity supply at the mains before starting work. Unscrew the wall-mounted light fitting, taking care to support its weight in the process.

2 Using insulating tape, cover the exposed wires. Replace the fitting's screws in the wall. It may be helpful to draw a diagram of the wiring layout to assist you when replacing the fitting later.

3 Paper over the area. Use a pencil to mark on the paper the location of the base of the wires. Pull the paper back and make a small cut where the wiring is to go through. Then pull the cable through the paper.

4 Using a paper-hanging brush, smooth the paper allowing the wall screws to break through the paper surface. Trim as necessary. Do not replace the fitting until the painting has been completed.

RADIATORS

A radiator roller is really a tool designed for painting, but its design makes it ideal for pushing paper down behind a central-heating radiator. With its soft, padded head there is no risk of tearing the damp, pasted paper.

1 When arriving at a radiator, place the paper over the top of it, keeping the butt join flush. Then carefully pull the paper away from the wall to reveal the radiator's supporting brackets.

2 Holding the length of paper over the front of the radiator, mark the location of the two supporting brackets with a pencil.

3 Using scissors, make a vertical cut from the bottom of the paper to the pencil mark. Do this for each supporting bracket.

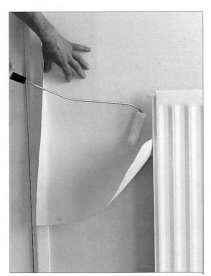

4 Using a radiator roller, push the paper into position on either side of the brackets, and wipe off any excess paste.

Cleaning up

Once papering has been completed, it is essential to spend time cleaning equipment and clearing up. It would be irritating to find stiff brushes, grimy buckets and paste-covered scissors when next starting a decorating job. You would immediately regret not clearing up properly last time, and may have to buy some new equipment.

Unused rolls of paper should be stored in a dry place, with part-used rolls bound with tape to prevent them unrolling and getting damaged.

TOOLS: Sponge, bucket with lid, nail

MATERIALS: Detergent, clean cloth, water

1 Wash the paper-hanging brush under warm running water using household detergent to remove any dry paste. Rinse thoroughly and allow to dry before storing. To clean the pasting brush, remove as much excess paste as possible from the bristles. Then wash, rinse and dry in the same way.

2 Rinse the paper-hanging scissors in warm water under the tap, sponging off any dry paste which would otherwise blunt the cutting edges. Make sure to thoroughly dry every part of the scissors with a clean cloth, to prevent any possibility of corrosion.

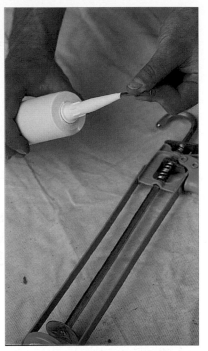

3 If you have overestimated the amount of paste required for the job, and are likely to need more in the near future, it can be stored for a few weeks in an airtight container.

4 Wipe the table with clean water and a sponge, paying particular attention to the edges where paste generally collects. Only fold up the table to store when it is completely dry.

5 It is important to seal a partly used tube of flexible filler so that it does not dry out and become impossible to use again. Place a nail in the end of the nozzle.

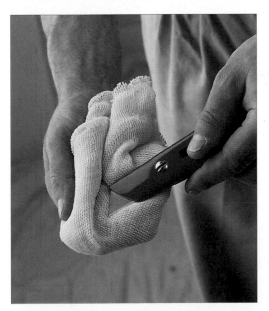

6 Before putting away a craft knife, it should be carefully wiped clean with a damp cloth to remove all traces of paste. Then dry it thoroughly. For obvious safety reasons, dispose of old blades – even if they are blunt – by placing them in a container such as an empty paint can. Make sure the can is sealed securely before putting it out with the rest of the rubbish. Metal objects such as these blades are recyclable, an option which should always be considered.

PASTE DISPOSAL
Most wallpaper paste contains fungicide and so is not biodegradable. Therefore, paste should never be tipped down a drain, as it may pollute nearby streams and water tables. Put it in a container that can be sealed before throwing it out.

Painting

With all the 'dirty' work done – sanding, filling, priming and general preparation – the actual painting can be the most enjoyable part of redecorating your home. This chapter demonstrates all the different techniques and methods for applying both undercoats and top coats, to all interior surfaces. Always remember to read the manufacturer's guidelines on the number of coats required for each particular type of paint, and use our recommendations on Order of Work (see pages 14–15). Allow adequate drying time between coats and never rush your work, as this will inevitably spoil the overall finish.

This chapter contains

Preparation

The order in which you carry out your work is very important as it will ensure that you do each particular task once. There is nothing more frustrating than having to repaint something because of bad planning. As a basic rule, paint the ceiling first, followed by the walls and then the woodwork. Keeping to this order will make sure that splashes from the ceiling to the walls and overlap from walls to woodwork will be covered by each subsequent stage of painting. When painting smaller items, such as window furniture, they should be considered as finishing touches and left until the end. Whether using solvent- or water-based paints, during every stage keep the doors and windows open in order to give adequate ventilation.

TOOLS: Dusting brush, lid opener, stirring stick, paint kettle, kitchen foil, gauze cloth, large rubber band, scraper

MATERIALS: Paint, masking tape

PREPARING THE PAINT

1 Before opening the paint can, use a dusting brush to wipe the lid clean, as grit and dirt tend to collect around the rim. If you do not do this, debris may fall into the paint as you remove the lid. Prise the lid open with a blunt instrument. A tool designed for this task can be bought cheaply and saves damaging expensive items such as screwdrivers or chisels.

2 Some paints, such as non-drip gloss and solid emulsion, must not be stirred before use, so always read the manufacturer's guidelines. Otherwise, most paints need a thorough stir. Use either a proprietary stirring stick or a piece of wooden dowel. As you stir, try to use a lifting motion. This brings up any sediment from the bottom of the can, and ensures that the pigments are mixed thoroughly.

3 It is advisable to decant the paint into a paint kettle for several reasons. First, the original paint can will stay cleaner for storage and for when it is next opened. Second, if the kettle is knocked over or dropped less paint is spilt, and finally, if any debris gets into the kettle it can be cleaned out and refilled from the original can. Lining a paint kettle with kitchen foil will save time when cleaning it out or using a different colour of paint.

4 When using paint left over from a previous job, you may find a skin has formed over the paint's surface. Remove this from the can before attempting to stir. The paint may still have lumps, so it is advisable to sieve the paint before use. Place some stockinette or gauze cloth over the paint kettle and hold it in place with a large rubber band. Pour the paint slowly into the kettle. The lumps will be sieved out of the paint.

NON-DRIP PAINTS

Solid emulsion and other non-drip paints have been created purely to make painting easier. They do not need stirring and they cause less mess during painting because of their special consistency.

MASKING

It is not always possible to remove the carpet from a room before decorating. Apply masking tape to the edge of the carpet, using a scraper to push it under the skirting board. The tape will stop carpet fluff getting on the new paintwork as well as keeping the paint off the carpet when you paint the skirting board. Remove the tape before the final coat hardens completely, or you may risk tearing the paint surface.

Using a roller

Using a roller is the quickest and most efficient way of covering large surface areas. Rollers can be used to apply solvent-based paints, but they are most often used with water-based paints such as emulsion or acrylic eggshell. Roller heads have become more varied in recent years with a range of sizes and textures, making them practically indispensable to the modern decorator.

TOOLS: Roller, roller tray, radiator roller, textured roller, extension pole, roller shield

MATERIALS: Paint, clingfilm

1 A roller tray consists of two parts: the paint reservoir, and a ribbed slope to wipe off excess paint and allow it to run back into the reservoir. Pour the prepared paint into the tray's reservoir, filling it to just below the start of the slope.

2 Dip the roller head into the paint reservoir and run it firmly up and down the ribs of the slope to distribute the paint evenly round the roller. Take care not to overload the head or paint will drip and splatter everywhere.

3 Move the loaded roller over the wall surface using light, even strokes. Working the roller too fast will cause a fine mist of paint spray, and should be avoided. Each time the roller is reloaded, apply it to an unpainted surface and then work back to the previously painted area in a series of overlapping strokes.

SPECIAL ROLLERS AND TOOLS

Extension poles

These are attached to the roller handle and are extremely effective when painting ceilings and stairwells. However, do not save them just for heights: an extension pole can also reduce the amount of bending necessary when reloading the roller, or when painting low areas.

Textured rollers

Textured paints are similar to very thick emulsion. They are excellent for covering up small cracks, and here a textured roller is used to create a stippled effect. The paint tends to dry quickly, so it is advisable to work in small areas of approximately 1sq m (1sq yd) at a time.

Roller shield

A roller with a plastic shield is a useful tool, especially when painting a ceiling. It helps avoid both roller spray and dripping from the edges of the roller frame. It can be added to an extension pole for painting ceilings, but check that it matches your pole before buying it.

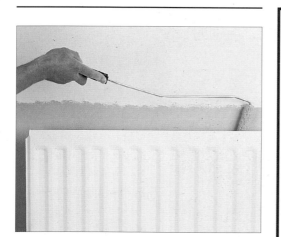

4 Work around and behind awkward areas such as pipes and radiators with a long-handled radiator roller. Without this special tool, these areas might otherwise be difficult to reach.

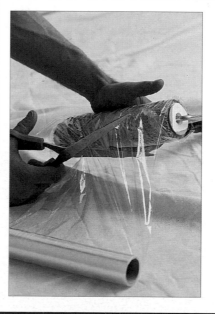

TEMPORARY STORAGE

When you have to pause during painting – between coats, for example – wrap a short length of clingfilm around the roller head, making sure to expel any trapped air. This saves having to wash out and dry the roller at frequent intervals.

Pads and sprayers

Paint pads, sprayers and spray guns are alternatives to the more traditional rollers and brushes.

Paint pads make less spray and mess than rollers. Their design has been improved in recent years, so now they can be used successfully, not just for covering large flat surfaces, but also for small, intricate areas such as window beads and door architraves.

Airless spray guns have also become more efficient and, on the whole, have dropped dramatically in price, making them a possibility for the home decorator. The technique for spraying can be mastered surprisingly quickly and can give a very satisfying and professional finish.

TOOLS: Paint pads, paint tray, paint sprayer, goggles, respirator mask, gloves, dust sheets

MATERIALS: Masking tape, paint

PAINT PADS

1 Paint pads are flat and rectangular with closely packed, short, fine fibres. They produce a smooth paint finish when used carefully. Pads come in a range of sizes for all-round use.

2 When loading a paint pad, gently dip the fibres into the tray reservoir. Take care not to immerse the pad head, as this will cause drips when it is used on the wall. Pull the pad over the ribbed slope to distribute the paint evenly. Some trays come with a built-in ribbed roller to remove the excess paint.

3 To paint the wall, use light even strokes in all directions, slightly overlapping each stroke. Pads need reloading more often than rollers as their fibres cannot hold as much paint. Paint pads tend to be faster than a brush but slower than a roller. There may be a need for extra coats as although pads apply paint very evenly, they tend to produce thinner coats. Extension poles can be attached to paint-pad heads to reach awkward areas such as ceilings.

PAINT SPRAYERS

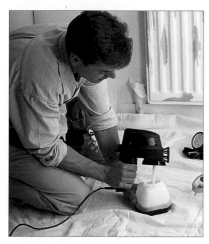

1 Mask up all the surrounding areas that are not to be painted. Thin the paint if necessary, following the manufacturer's guidelines, and pour into the reservoir of the spray gun. Attach the reservoir to the gun and select the correct nozzle for the type of paint and finish required.

2 It is wise to test the spray gun and your spraying technique on some old newspaper before starting the particular job in hand. As the paint spray may spatter slightly when the gun is started, first spray slightly away from the area that is to be painted, and then slowly sweep across the actual area.

3 As you progress, use a steady deliberate motion, slightly overlapping the paint that has been already applied. Never be tempted to return to a patchy area: the paint may run because too much has been applied in one coat. Many thin coats are definitely preferable to one or two thick ones.

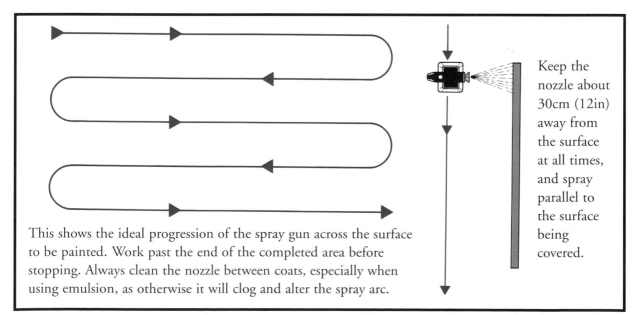

This shows the ideal progression of the spray gun across the surface to be painted. Work past the end of the completed area before stopping. Always clean the nozzle between coats, especially when using emulsion, as otherwise it will clog and alter the spray arc.

Keep the nozzle about 30cm (12in) away from the surface at all times, and spray parallel to the surface being covered.

Using a brush

Brushes have long been the most popular and adaptable tools for painting nearly all surfaces. A brush has been designed to cope with almost every problem, from large areas to seemingly unreachable gaps behind radiators. Pure bristle brushes are still the professional choice, although synthetic alternatives are available. Brush prices vary considerably, but it is worth paying a little extra for quality. Cheaper options tend to be stiffer with shorter bristles, and moult continually, making a good finish hard to achieve.

TOOLS: 100–125mm (4–5in) paintbrush, paint kettle, vacuum cleaner, paint shield

MATERIALS: Paint, clean cloth, white spirit

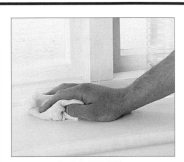

1 Before starting to paint, flick the end of the brush and wipe it on a lint-free cloth to remove any loose bristles and dust. New brushes should be used to prime or undercoat wood to get rid of bristles which are often loosened when they are first used. Such brushes can then be used for top coats at a later date.

2 Dip the brush into the paint so that about one-third of the bristles are immersed. Raise the brush and gently push the bristles against the side of the paint kettle to get rid of excess paint. Avoid scraping the brush on the edge of the kettle as this will build up paint on the inside and form drips down the outside.

FINAL CLEANING
Even after thorough preparation and cleaning down of surfaces to be painted, dust can still accumulate on horizontal areas such as window sills. Just before painting, wipe them with a lint-free cloth dampened with a little white spirit. They will dry quickly by evaporation, leaving completely dust-free surfaces on which an excellent finish can be achieved.

3 When using water-based paint on a large area such as a wall, choose a 100–125mm (4–5 in) paintbrush, as one that is any larger will be heavy and will quickly tire your arm. Apply the paint to the wall with short, overlapping horizontal and vertical strokes. Work in areas of approximately 1sq m (1sq yd) at a time.

4 With the brush unloaded, remove any visible brush marks by lightly drawing the bristles across the painted surface, again using a series of horizontal and vertical strokes. This technique is known as 'laying off'. Having completed this process, move on to the adjoining area, always working away from the wet edge.

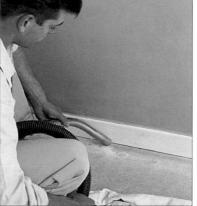

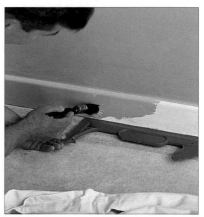

5 When applying solvent-based paint to a large area, make three vertical, parallel strips of about 30cm (12in) long. Without reloading the brush, blend the strips together horizontally, brushing out the paint. To complete the laying-off process finish with light vertical strokes .

6 Always try to keep the decorating area as clean and dust free as possible. A vacuum cleaner is the most efficient way of keeping the room clean, and is especially useful at skirting-board level. If any dirt or grit is picked up on the skirting board, sand it lightly between coats.

7 When painting the skirting board, place a paint shield or a clean piece of cardboard against the bottom, parallel to the floorboards or carpet. This will ensure that no dirt is picked up from the floor by the brush and transferred to the painted surface. It will also protect the flooring.

Cutting in

Although rollers and paint pads are efficient for covering large areas such as walls and ceilings, it is still necessary to finish the job off around the edges. This is known as 'cutting in' or beading.

When using a roller, for example, you can cut in either before or after doing the rollering, as long as the paint edges are still wet when either process is carried out. This is because wet and dry paint edges, on the same coat, can cause an unsightly framing effect. When drying conditions are quick (normally with all water-based paints), take each ceiling or wall at a time, completing it before going on to the next area, thus keeping paint edges wet at all times.

TOOLS: 50–60mm (2–2½ in) paintbrush, fitch, corner roller, small paint pad,

MATERIALS: Paint, clean cloth, white spirit, masking tape

CORNERS

1 When cutting in up to an already painted surface, it will be necessary to bead the paint up to the corner very precisely, in order to produce the required finish. A 50–60mm (2–2½in) brush is an ideal size for this job. Load the brush and apply a 50cm (20in) strip of paint, slightly away from the corner.

2 With the brush (now unloaded) spread the paint up to the corner junction, using the splayed edge of the bristles. Bead the paint right into the corner creating a neat, straight line. For extra precision, you may need to repeat this process two or three times to move the paint exactly into the junction.

3 In the corner of the room, or a tight angle near built-in furniture, etc, it is sometimes easiest to use a small, flat, angle-headed fitch rather than an ordinary paintbrush, however small. The finer angled bristles make it easier to get right into the corner and give a finish that is totally neat and squared.

FITTINGS

1 When cutting in around small obstacles such as electrical sockets and light switches, a fitch is often more precise and therefore easier to use than a larger brush.

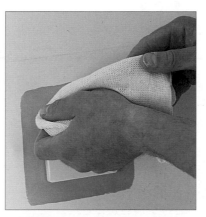

2 Take care to remove any paint marks on the socket while they are still wet. Use a cloth slightly dampened with either water or white spirit, depending on the type of paint.

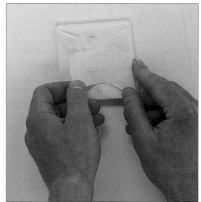

3 Although more time consuming, masking tape can also be used to cover fittings. If the fitting is intricate or difficult to clean, this option should be considered seriously.

4 Along an edge where both painted surfaces will be the same colour, a corner roller may be used as an alternative to cutting in with a brush. Take care not to overload the roller with paint as this will almost certainly leave unsightly roller trails and give varying thicknesses of paint that will detract from the finish.

5 Small paint pads give an excellent straight edge when cutting in to a surface of a different colour. Line up the pad's top edge against the ceiling and draw it across the wall. However, pads are not suitable if the corner is uneven or undulating: they are not very flexible and cannot bead exactly into the corner.

OVERLAPPING EDGES

Notice how, in this example, the ceiling paint was overlapped on to the wall. This is standard procedure as it is pointless to cut in precisely into a corner with both paint colours. The second colour will always cover up such overlaps, therefore saving time.

Doors

Doors get more wear and tear than any other painted area in the home. Solvent-based paints are most often used to cope with the needs of frequently used surfaces, because they are particularly hard-wearing. The basic rule for painting doors is to stick to a logical sequence.

Remove all door furniture before starting as this avoids having to cut in around it. This is also an ideal opportunity to either paint or clean decorative door furniture.

TOOLS: 25, 50 and 75mm (1, 2 and 3in) paintbrushes, paint kettle

MATERIALS: Paint

FLUSH DOOR

1 Mentally divide the door into eight sections, and starting in the top left-hand corner, work from left to right and downwards. Use a 50–75mm (2–3in) brush for quick coverage and therefore to avoid the danger of tide marks. Take care not to overload the wet edges of each section as this can easily lead to runs and paint sagging.

2 As each section of the door is covered, make a series of light upward strokes with the brush to lay off the paint. Once it is all complete, use a smaller brush to paint the edges of the door, plus the door frame and the architrave, using the diagram on page 75 as a guideline for exactly which areas to paint.

Colour divisions on a door and doorway

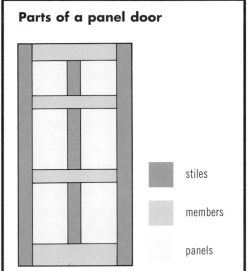

frame head

architrave

hanging edge

door stop

Colours for room A

Colours for room B

Parts of a panel door

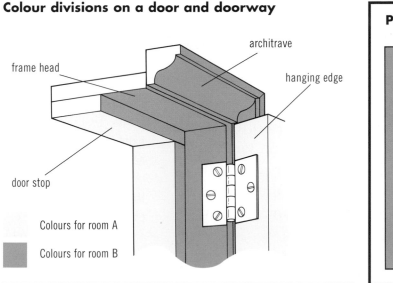

stiles

members

panels

PANEL DOOR

1 Using a 50mm (2in) brush, begin with the top panels, doing the mouldings first. Work down, completing all the panels in sequence. Paint runs often occur at the panel corners, so it may be necessary to brush them out, returning to them several times.

2 Again starting from the top of the door, paint the central vertical stiles. Take care not to brush too far on to the horizontal members (the areas between the panels) as the vertical brush marks may show through on the final coat.

3 When the central vertical stiles are completed, paint the three horizontal members, always remembering to lay off the paint in the natural direction of the grain of the wood.

4 Paint the outer vertical stiles. Then, using a smaller brush, paint the door edges. Try to avoid getting paint on the hinges. Last, paint the door frame and architrave. Remember to wedge the door open while it dries.

Casement windows

Windows can be fiddly to paint, but by working in an organised way you can keep frustration to a minimum, and achieve a good result. Doing a thorough job on windows is particularly important: of all areas in the home, they are most affected by exterior climatic changes. Direct sunlight and condensation, as well as minor expansion and contraction of joints all take their toll.

Paint windows early in the day so they do not have to stay open all night to dry.

TOOLS: Screwdrivers, 35mm (1½in) paintbrush, paint kettle, small angle-headed brush

MATERIALS: Paint, clean cloth, masking tape

Parts of a casement window

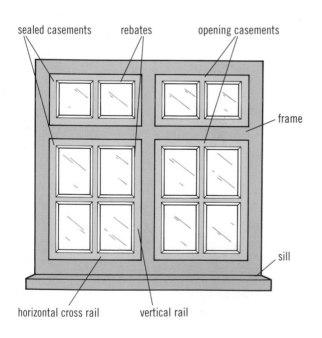

sealed casements rebates opening casements

frame

sill

horizontal cross rail vertical rail

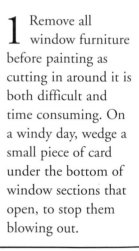

1 Remove all window furniture before painting as cutting in around it is both difficult and time consuming. On a windy day, wedge a small piece of card under the bottom of window sections that open, to stop them blowing out.

4 Having finished all sections of the window that open, paint all the non-opening parts around the panes of glass. This completes all fiddly, small sections.

METAL WINDOWS

Metal windows that are normally painted are prepared and repainted in exactly the same way as their wooden counterparts. However, if there are any patches of rust, they should be cleaned back thoroughly to the sound, bare metal and initially treated with metal primer.

Aluminium and PVC windows are specifically designed to require very little maintenance. They should not be painted. To keep them clean and bright, wash them down during decoration with warm soapy water. Never use abrasive cleaners on either aluminium or PVC as they may scratch and disfigure the surface.

MASKING WINDOW PANES

Although time consuming, masking up individual panes is one way to keep paint off the glass surface. This is a particularly good option for the beginner, and can be discarded when your beading/cutting-in technique has been mastered. If you do mask the panes, remember to remove the tape when the top coat is still tacky, otherwise you may tear the painted surface.

2 Mentally divide the window into smaller sections, and begin by painting all the parts that open. As usual, start right at the top of the window. This example shows the small opener being painted first.

3 Paint the lower opening sections of the window. With each separate section, paint the window rebates first and work out to the cross rails and vertical rails.

5 Finish off by painting the larger parts: the outer window frame and the sill. Keep returning to the window to check for paint runs, which are especially common at the rebate–rail junctions.

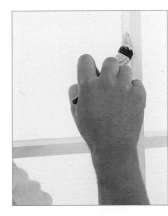

6 Painting window rebates needs a technique similar to cutting in (see page 72). Again it is necessary to bead the paint right up to the wood–glass junction. This can be made easier by using a small angle-headed brush.

Sash windows

Due to their design, sash windows appear to be difficult to paint, but if the correct sequence of painting is followed, they are as straightforward as any other painting job.

If the runners are in sound, painted condition they are best left alone, as too many coats of paint will make the window jam. It is also important to keep paint away from the sash cords, so they can run freely.

TOOLS: Fitch, 50mm (2in) paintbrush, paint kettle, window guard, window scraper

MATERIALS: Paint, masking tape

Parts of a sash window

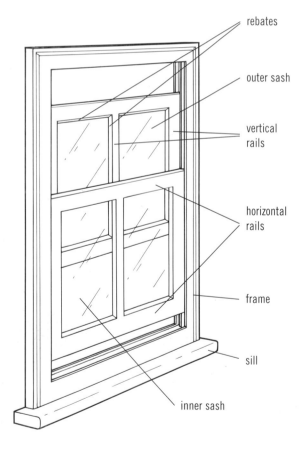

rebates

outer sash

vertical rails

horizontal rails

frame

sill

inner sash

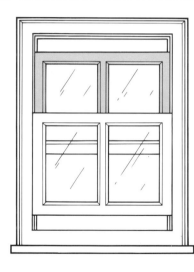

1 Open the window slightly at both top and bottom, and start by painting the top half of the outer sash rebates. Move on to the horizontal and vertical rails.

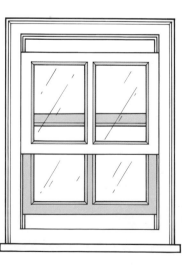

2 Raise the inner sash until it is nearly at the top of the frame and pull down the outer sash. Finish off painting the rebates, horizontal and vertical rails on the outer sash. Then paint the inner sash rebates.

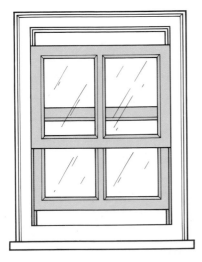

3 Leave the sashes in the same position as step 2, and finish painting the inner sash. Then paint the exposed lower runners, taking care not to touch or smudge the wet paint just applied to either of the sashes.

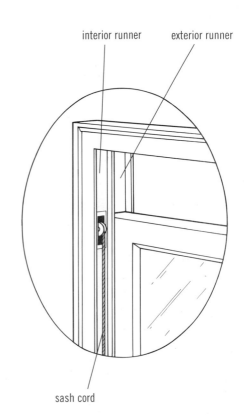

Parts of a sash window – mechanism

interior runner exterior runner

sash cord

4 Return the window to its original position (step 1) and paint the upper runners. The top and bottom edges of the inner sash can now be painted. Finally, paint the surrounding frame and sill.

IDEAL TOOLS

Window guards

Saves time by keeping paint off the glass. Hold the guard tight up against the glass and the rebate, paint around the pane and move the guard along to the next area. Window guards are less effective on older widows, as undulating rebates and small joint variations allow paint to squeeze out under the guard's edges. Wipe it clean frequently to avoid paint build-up and smudging.

Window scraper

Handy for removing paint overspill or spray from the glass of the window once the paint has dried.

Fitch

Useful for painting the runners as it is important to keep paint clear of the sash cord, otherwise the sliding mechanism will be hampered.

Metal

Household fixtures and fittings are made from a variety of metals. For example, central-heating radiators are commonly made from ferrous metals whereas copper pipes and aluminium are non-ferrous and do not corrode as much. Window and door furniture may be made from either of these types.

Remove as much metalwork as possible from doors and windows. This will make painting both the main object and the metal fitting much easier.

TOOLS: Fitch, 37 and 50mm (1½ and 2in) paintbrushes, paint kettle, wire brush, scraper, screwdriver

MATERIALS: Heat-resistant, solvent-based and aerosol paints, wire wool, clean cloth, wooden battens

HEATED METAL SURFACES

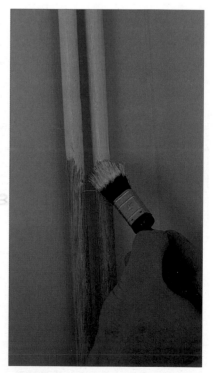

1 Always prepare and paint an object that gets hot, when it is cold. Otherwise the paint will dry too quickly, producing an uneven, blotchy finish. On cast iron, such as a wood-burning stove or a fire surround, use a wire brush to remove any loose material, then dust off. Wipe down using a cloth dampened with white spirit to remove any remaining particles.

2 Because a cast-iron stove or fireplace may reach a very high temperature when it is being used, apply a paint specifically manufactured for heated cast-iron surfaces. Paints that are not heat resistant would burn and bubble off. A primer is not usually necessary with such specialist paints and two full-strength coats, painted or sprayed on, should be sufficient.

3 For pipes and radiators, solvent-based paints are best as most water-based paints will discolour with the heat.

DOOR AND WINDOW FITTINGS

1 Tarnish and spots of paint can be cleaned off most window furniture with fine-grade wire wool. However, this method may scratch or abrade some surfaces, so try a small test area first. Alternatively, use the edge of a scraper to remove old paint.

2 Some window furniture can be rejuvenated or blended into your chosen colour scheme by being sprayed with aerosol paint. Check that the paint is suitable for the type of metal, and raise the items up on a couple of wooden battens to give access to all sides when spraying.

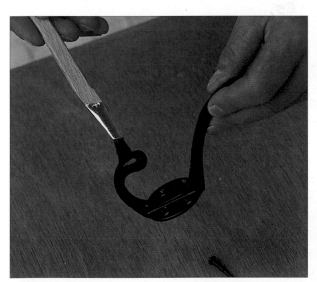

3 Alternatively, paint such objects using a small fitch. Placing them on a clean board will prevent them sticking to dust sheets while drying.

4 Do not paint the screws before reattaching the fitting as a screwdriver will damage the paint. Simply 'touch in' the screw heads once replaced.

Floors

Painting a concrete floor is an inexpensive way to clean up and give colour to what would otherwise be a dull, dusty surface. A new concrete floor should be left to dry out for up to six months before painting.

Wooden flooring can be split into two broad categories: blocks and planking. Both types need to be sealed to provide a practical, usable surface. Although there is a wide variety of finishes available, all wooden floors are prepared in the same way.

TOOLS: Broom, 100mm (4in) paintbrush, paint kettle, hammer, nail punch, floor sander, floor polisher

MATERIALS: Cement mix, clean cloth, white spirit, floor paint, wax/oil/varnish

CONCRETE FLOORS

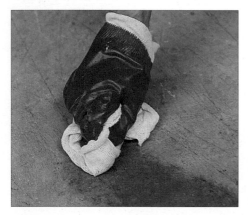

1 Sweep the concrete floor with a soft brush to remove all the dirt and debris. Fill any cracks or holes with a cement mix and allow to dry. Wipe the floor with a damp cloth to ensure that it is dust free. Oil and grease marks should be removed using a cleaning solvent such as white spirit. If there is no skirting board, overlap the wall paint on to the floor by 5cm (2in) to make it easier to achieve a neat, straight line at the edges when using the floor paint.

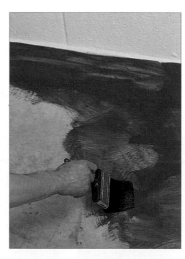

2 Remember to open all windows and doors to provide good ventilation, to get rid of fumes and to speed up drying. Thin the first coat of the floor paint with white spirit, carefully following the manufacturer's instructions. Thinning allows the paint to soak into the concrete, sealing the surface. Always work back towards the door so you don't get stuck in a corner.

3 Allow the first, thinned coat of paint to dry thoroughly. Then apply a further two coats of full-strength floor paint. While the floor is drying it will be tacky and will mark easily, so keep doors shut to prevent children and pets from straying on to the painted surface.

WOODEN FLOORS

1 Use a nail punch to punch in any protruding nails, and fix any loose boards. Always start a sander tilted back to avoid damaging the floor while the sander is stationary. Sand along the grain, starting with a coarse-grade paper and finishing with a fine-grade. On old floors, be sure to remove all traces of previous treatments to get a sound base on which to begin.

USING AN INDUSTRIAL SANDER

Large, industrial sanders are reasonably inexpensive to hire and save a large amount of time when preparing a wooden floor. However, they are extremely noisy and dusty, so ear protectors, goggles and a dust mask are essential. Open all the windows to maximise ventilation, but it may be worth running masking tape around the internal doorways to keep dust out of the rest of the house.

A large sander cannot get within about 5cm (2in) of a wall. Once you have sanded the main part of the floor, the edges have to be finished off with a smaller, hand-held sander.

2 Vacuum the area free of dust, wipe the floor using a cloth dampened with white spirit and allow to dry. A sealing coat may then be applied. Wax, as shown here, should be worked well into the grain using a lint-free cloth.

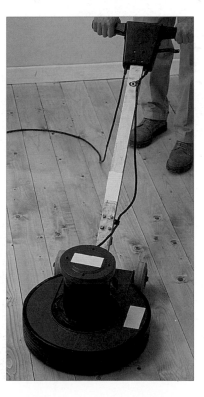

3 Once the wax has dried, use an electric floor polisher to buff the surface. Keep applying coats until a deep sheen is achieved. A natural wax floor may need many applications to reach the desired effect, but its look will continue to improve as it ages.

Staining and varnishing

These sealing coats are designed both to protect bare wood and to enhance its natural grain and pattern. However, because they are quite translucent, any small defects in the wood will show through the finished surface. Therefore, before applying any type of stain or varnish, take extra time to check that every surface has been prepared thoroughly and all marks, or traces of previous paint, have been completely removed.

Work without interruption if possible, as keeping a wet edge is important to avoid unsightly brush marks.

TOOLS: Varnish brushes, paint kettle

MATERIALS: Varnish, wood stain, white spirit, sandpaper, clean cloth

STAINING

1 Staining tends to give more dramatic colouring than varnishing, and is ideal to blend different types of wood together. When staining a door use the same order of work as for painting (see pages 74–75). Take extra care not to overlap sections or to allow drips to occur as this will show in the final result. For this reason it is best to work with the door flat, making sure that the other side of the door is adequately padded to prevent damaging it.

2 Brush the stain well into the grain, regularly checking that no surface build-up has occurred. Subsequent coats of stain should be applied, not only to increase hard-wearing properties but also to build up the depth of colour in the wood.

VARNISHING

1 When using solvent-based varnish on bare wood, the first coat should be thinned, using 10 parts varnish to 1 part of solvent, and used as a primer/sealer. Apply using a lint-free cloth rubbing well into, and in the direction of, the natural grain. Acrylic varnishes may be brushed on direct, without thinning.

2 Allow to dry, and use a fine-grade sandpaper to gently smooth down the surface, removing any dust or grit. Wipe the surface clean using a cloth dampened with white spirit.

3 Use a clean brush to apply the next coat of varnish. Do not overload the brush, and brush the varnish well into the grain using even strokes. Several coats should be applied to attain a long-lasting finish. Lightly sand and clean down between coats.

3 Treat the vertical stiles and the horizontal members of a panelled door as though they are quite separate parts, making clean straight lines at their joints with the stain. This prevents brush marks in the wrong direction showing on either area and ruining the clear-cut look of the natural grain.

4 Drips are sometimes unavoidable but should be dealt with quickly before they dry. Check for drips regularly during the drying process, brushing them away immediately.

SEPARATE BRUSHES

Brushes used for paint tend to bleed colour which will effect a varnished finish. Therefore keep separate varnish and painting brushes.

Waxing and oiling

Wood is fed and nourished by waxes and oils. They stop it from drying out and cracking – a common problem in modern centrally heated homes – and provide a different feel and texture from the more commonly used sealing stains and varnishes.

Oil is a particularly effective finish for hardwoods such as oak or ash and will revive even the most faded worn areas, restoring them to their former glory. On bare wood, two coats of wax are adequate, but further coats will build up depth of colour and sheen.

For further information on the application of waxes and oils, see pages 14–15.

TOOLS: 25 and 37mm (1 and 1½in) paintbrushes, paint kettle

MATERIALS: Sandpaper, oil, lint-free cloth, wax, dye

OILING

1 Prepare the bare wood as usual (see pages 32–33), and apply the oil sparingly, using a.brush or cloth.

2 After a few minutes, use a lint-free cloth to wipe off any surplus oil that has not soaked into the wood. Areas that are subjected to heavy wear, such as floors, may need several applications of the oil.

FIRE RISK
Old oiled cloths and rags are highly flammable. After use they should be soaked in water, sealed in an old paint can and disposed of safely

WAXING

1 Thoroughly sand all surfaces, working along the grain where possible. In more intricate areas, such as the mouldings of a bannister rail (as pictured), it may be easier to use the sandpaper rolled up like a tube. Dust off and wipe down all areas using a cloth dampened with white spirit.

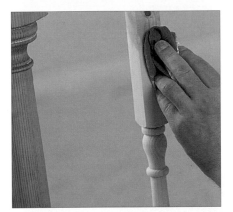

2 Apply the wax with a lint-free cloth, working it along the grain of the wood. Do not worry unduly about obtaining a completely streak-free finish as any unsightly marks or build-up of the wax will soon disappear when the surface is buffed and polished.

3 For areas of finer detail a cloth is not always the best tool for the job. Use a small brush to get into awkward areas.

COLOUR CHECKS

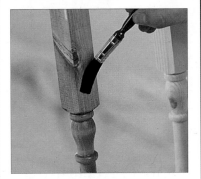

Most waxes contain their own pigmentation, so it is wise to try a small test area out of sight before waxing an entire surface. Using a wood dye before applying wax is an alternative way to colour the wood. Wood dyes may be applied using a brush or cloth. The majority can be mixed with each other allowing many choices of colour. Again, test a small area to check the colour.

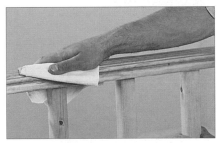

4 After approximately 15 minutes, buff off the waxed areas with a soft clean cloth, again working along the grain where possible. Fine-grade steel wool may also be used for this purpose. Apply further coats, using the same technique.

Problems and faults

All manner of problems and faults may occur during painting or after it has been completed. Most can be put down to poor preparation, incompatible paints, rushed work or a badly done job. Always remember to read the manufacturer's guidelines for each specific coating, and never try to cut corners. Some problems can be rectified more easily than others. The most common are outlined below.

POOR COVERAGE

Usually found where a solvent-based gloss has been applied over the wrong undercoat, or even no undercoat at all. Sand back and apply the correct paint that should have been used at first. With water-based paints, it is usually due to insufficient coats of paint. Adding extra coats will normally solve the problem.

MISCELLANEOUS STAINS

Damp patches, rust spots or bleeding bitumen are most often found 'grinning' through emulsion or water-based paints, as solvent-based paints will often cover such problems. Apply a stain block, allow it to dry, and repaint the surface. For persistent damp stains or unidentifiable marks, consult a professional.

ROLLER TRAILS

Occur in uneven areas because the roller is unable to run across the surface smoothly. As well, they can be caused by applying too much pressure to the roller while it is moving. Lightly sand back and repaint.

ORANGE PEEL/WRINKLING

Caused when a solvent-based paint has been applied over a first coat of paint that has not completely dried. Strip the paint back to the bare surface and repaint, allowing adequate drying time between coats.

DRIPS AND RUNS

Occur when too much paint has been used on a vertical surface. Allow the paint to dry completely, sand back to remove the runs and get a smooth surface, and repaint.

GRIT OR DIRT

Caused either by poor initial preparation of surfaces or by dirt being picked up by the brush while painting. Lightly sand back, wipe down with a dampened cloth and repaint.

BRUSH MARKS

Caused by general over application or lack of 'laying off' when painting. Usually worst with wood stain. To solve the problem, with both paint and wood stain, the area must be sanded back completely or even stripped, in severe cases. Then reapply the paint or stain.

BLISTERING/BUBBLING

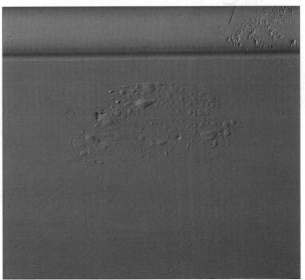

Occurs when moisture or air is trapped beneath the paint and has expanded due to heat. Strip back to the bare wood, fill any holes and repaint. Similar-looking bubbles can occur with water-based paints on plaster. This is due to poor preparation or dusty surfaces. Sand back, prepare correctly and repaint.

Cleaning up and storage

Once the job is complete, all equipment should be cleaned thoroughly before being put away. Do not make the common mistake of leaving brushes in a jar of white spirit and expecting them to be as good as new in six months' time, as they will simply dry out and be ruined. There are obvious savings to be made by looking after expensive brushes and rollers. Although the process may seem arduous at the time, you will be grateful when you come to tackle the next decorating project.

   Remember to dispose of any empty cans or chemical debris safely.

TOOLS: Scraper, craft knife

MATERIALS: Household detergent, wire wool, white spirit, glass jar, clean cloth, brown paper, rubber band, hand cleanser

WATER-BASED PAINT

1 Clean rollers or pads by first wiping off the excess on an old board or some newspaper. Then wash the pad or roller sleeve under running water until the water runs clear. This is aided by the use of a mild household detergent. Rinse and shake dry.

2 Wash out brushes using the same technique for rollers or pads. To remove any dried paint, a blunt scraper can be drawn across the bristles. Wire wool is useful to remove paint from the ferrule or from a metal roller cage which often becomes caked in paint.

CLEANING HANDS
Many decorating products may irritate the skin, so adequate protection, such as gloves, should always be worn. However, splashes of paint are sometimes unavoidable. To clean them off, use a proprietary hand cleanser.

SOLVENT-BASED PAINT

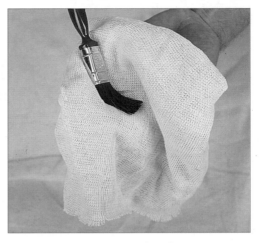

2 Take the brush out, removing the excess cleaning agent by drawing the bristles across the edge of the jar. Dry the brush thoroughly with a clean

1 Remove any excess paint from the brush and stir it vigorously in a jar of white spirit or proprietary brush cleaner.

cloth. Repeat steps 1 and 2 if excess paint is still evident in the bristles. Finally, wash with warm water and detergent, rinse and shake dry.

CLEANING SYSTEM BOX

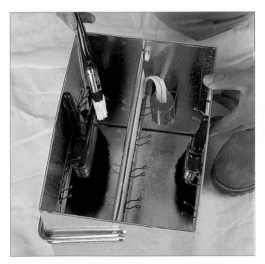

As an alternative to cleaning out brushes which have been used with solvent-based products, a proprietary cleaning-system box may be used. Brushes can be stored indefinitely by suspending the drying process. Chemical vapour contained in such an enclosed space allows the bristles to remain moist and ready for use.

REMOVING PAINT FROM CARPET

Once the job is complete and the room returned to normal, it is not uncommon to find that the odd drop of paint has managed to find its way through the dust sheets and on to the carpet. Once the paint has dried out, small spots can be removed with a sharp craft knife. Do not cut downwards, but carefully scrape the carpet fibres across the surface of the carpet. You will be amazed how the paint disappears.

STORAGE

All brushes should be dry before they are put away. In order to keep them in prime condition, wrap the bristles in brown paper held in place with a rubber band. This will help the brush to keep its shape rather than allowing the bristles to splay out in all directions.

Glossary

Batten
A length of straight wood, used as a guideline.

Beading
Using the extreme edge of a paintbrush to achieve a precise dividing line between two colours.

Butt join
A join where two edges of wallpaper or lining paper meet exactly, but do not overlap.

Casement window
A window made up of hinged and/or fixed lights.

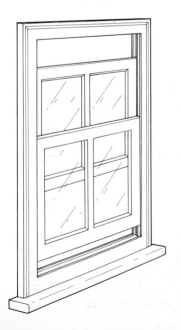

Ceiling rose
An electrical fitting found on ceilings through which a lighting pendant hangs.

Concertina
Wallpaper or lining paper that has been folded into manageable lengths, usually after pasting.

Cutting in
Painting into an angle such as between a wall or ceiling, or on to a narrow surface such as a glazing bar.

Distemper
Old-fashioned water-based paint.

Double lining
Two layers of lining paper, used to achieve a smooth finish on a rough surface.

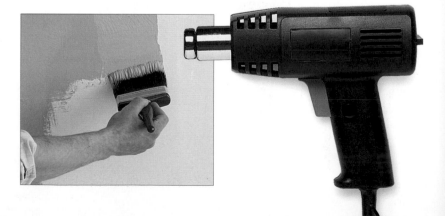

Feathering
Blending in uneven edges during sanding.

Ferrule
The metal band on a paintbrush that holds the bristles on to the handle.

Flush
Term used to describe two level, adjacent surfaces.

Fungicide
A chemical that kills mould.

Key
A slightly rough surface that has been sanded to provide a bond for paint or paper.

Laying off

Light brush strokes, made in a similar direction, to eliminate brush marks left on a painted surface.

Lining paper

Plain paper that gives a smooth surface on walls and ceilings prior to painting or hanging wall coverings.

Lint-free cloth

A cloth, usually made of cotton, which does not moult fibres.

Manufactured butt join

The process of overlapping wall coverings, cutting through both layers of paper and removing the excess strips to create a flush butt join.

Members

Horizontal wooden struts that are part of a panelled door.

Primer

Thinned, specially formulated paint that seals and stabilises a surface before undercoat is used.

Proud

Protruding slightly from the surrounding surface.

Rails

The horizontal and vertical struts in a window.

Rebate

The part of a rail that is at right angles to the pane of glass.

Recessed window

A window that is flush with the external wall thus creating a recess inside a room.

Size

A stabilising compound applied to porous surfaces to seal them before paper hanging.

Stiles

Vertical struts that are part of a panelled door.

Sash window

A window in which the opening sections – the sashes – slide up and down vertically within a frame, counterbalanced by weights held on sash cords.

Index